Cincinnati Seasoned

Savoring the Queen City's Spice of Life

JUNIOR LEAGUE OF CINCINNATI

Devou Park

William P. and Charles P. Devou had no idea what kind of view they would bestow on Greater Cincinnati. The brothers donated 500 acres of land to the City of Covington a hundred years ago in the hopes the city would create a park. All these years later, people love driving up the hill and bringing a camera along to snap a shot of Cincinnati's spectacular skyline.

Devou Park has a long tradition of offering outdoor recreation to the masses. In 1922 Covington officials celebrated the opening of a nine-hole golf course. The Covington Rotary Club took the rolling green space under its wings ten years later and began to improve the park by planting trees honoring their fallen loved ones. Rotary members launched three major projects in 1938, including a shelter house, two swimming pools, and a band shell. Since then, neighbors have enjoyed concerts and dramas, as well as ongoing performances by the Northern Kentucky Symphony.

The original shelter house was demolished in 1956 to make way for a new facility called the Memorial Building. The facility was built on top of the hill, giving people interested in public rental the one of the best vantage points in the region.

In 2003 the Drees Company donated a new reception and banquet facility to replace the Memorial Building. The $2 million building was dedicated in 2004, complete with a time capsule sealed in the brick. Today, people come to Devou Park to enjoy hiking, biking, and walking trails, a fishing lake, and the Behringer-Crawford Museum of Kentucky Heritage.

A nonprofit board manages the Pavilion and its profits, all with the goal to support future endeavors at Devou Park.

Discover the view at Drees Pavilion at Devou Park by visiting www.dreespavilion.com.

Cincinnati Seasoned

Savoring the Queen City's Spice of Life

JUNIOR LEAGUE OF CINCINNATI

Cincinnati Seasoned
Savoring the Queen City's Spice of Life

Published by Junior League of Cincinnati
Copyright © 2010
Junior League of Cincinnati
3500 Columbia Parkway
Cincinnati, Ohio 45226
513-871-9339

Food and Tablescape Photography © by Shad Ramsey
Historic Photography © by the Junior League of Cincinnati

Library of Congress Control Number: 2009924358
ISBN: 978-0-9607078-3-6

Edited, Designed, and Produced by

Favorite Recipes® Press
An imprint of

FRP. INC

A wholly owned subsidiary of Southwestern/Great American, Inc.
P.O. Box 305142
Nashville Tennessee 37230
800-358-0560

Art Director and Book Design: Starletta Polster
Project Editor: Tanis Westbrook

Manufactured in the United States of America
First Printing: 2010
15,000 copies

Mission

The Junior League of Cincinnati is an organization of women committed to promoting voluntarism, developing the potential of women, and improving communities through the effective action and leadership of trained volunteers. Its purpose is exclusively educational and charitable.

The Junior League of Cincinnati is an exclusively educational, charitable organization which reaches out to women of all races, religions, or national origins who demonstrate an interest in and commitment to voluntarism.

Vision Statement

The Junior League of Cincinnati is committed to improving our community by stimulating change and empowering people through the direct efforts of our dedicated volunteers. Our members are global in complexion and perspective. Partnerships with the community strengthen our ability to make an impact on the lives of those we serve.

Focus Area

Strengthening Childhood Environments

Belief Statement

We believe children need opportunities that foster self-confidence and success.
We believe children need the respect and support of a responsible role model.
We believe children need to be encouraged to read and write.

Membership / Organization

Founded in 1920, the Junior League of Cincinnati is part of a network of more than 294 Junior League Organizations in the United States, Canada, Mexico, and Great Britain. The Association of Junior League International, founded in 1901, has more than 170,000 members.

Training

A critical part of the JLC experience is to provide training opportunities for members. Topics are designed to focus on leadership, personal, and professional development.

2008–2009
Cookbook Committee

Katy Crossen
Co-chair,
Design and
Development

Tiffany Heath
Co-chair,
Marketing and
Sponsorship

Caroline Colvin
Karolyn Engler
Ramona Fahlbusch
Shelli French
Meredith Gorentz
Stephanie Greis
Heather Jackson
Allison Lied
Jessica Shelly
Liz Stoffregen

The Junior League of Cincinnati's first fund-raiser at Sinton Ballroom—1926

Dear Friend,

Every significant project is a labor of love, and *Cincinnati Seasoned* is no exception.

Having both grown up in Greater Cincinnati, we wanted to create a cookbook celebrating everything that is special about the Queen City—its rich history, its strong tradition of enjoying good food, and of course, our beloved Junior League of Cincinnati.

After getting acquainted on a very long drive to the Cookbook University seminar in Nashville, we both agreed we needed to commit a lot of time and energy to develop a cookbook worthy of such a remarkable community. We thought this "tablescape" concept was a perfect way to tie food to our best-loved landmarks, and we hope you agree. We strived to showcase some of the most recognizable places and spaces with unique touches you might not expect to see in a cookbook. We hope you find a photo of your favorite landmark in these pages.

This book also contains some of the most stunning dishes worthy of any dinner party or family gathering. We are so grateful to the many, many people who submitted hundreds of recipes to the Junior League of Cincinnati. Our thanks also go out to the many "chefs" who took on the daunting task of testing these recipes. Together, these efforts enabled us to put together a delicious representation of simple but sophisticated recipes that anyone can prepare.

Finally, we cannot express enough gratitude to the Junior League of Cincinnati leadership, Sustainers, Actives, and Provisionals who supported this project from its inception. The release of this book is intended to coincide with the 90th anniversary of our League, and we were determined to celebrate the vast commitment our organization has made to the Queen City. After much digging in the archives and dedicated assistance by the staff at Columbia Center, we were delighted to find historic photos of JLC members in action in the organization's first days. We hope you enjoy this beautiful trip down memory lane.

Cincinnati Seasoned was developed with much love and care, and we hope that sentiment comes out in the dishes you prepare for your treasured family and friends.

Cheers!

Katy Crossen & Tiffany Heath
JLC Cookbook Co-chairs, 2008–2009, 2009–2010

Miss Marjorie Gibson volunteering at Children's Convalescent Hospital

Dear Friend,

The Junior League of Cincinnati (JLC) has been a driving force in the Cincinnati community for an astounding ninety years. The very first Junior League was convened in New York in 1901 by founder Mary Harriman. Since the establishment of the Cincinnati chapter in 1920, we have stayed true to her vision of improving our communities by using the energy and commitment of women trained to be volunteers.

Across the nation, Junior Leagues have a rich history of publishing cookbooks. The book you are holding, *Cincinnati Seasoned*, is the fourth the JLC has launched. The proceeds will enable us to support our current projects, which all focus on strengthening childhood environments.

Over the years, the JLC has been instrumental in establishing a variety of community, cultural, and educational programs. Our largest visible gift to the community has been the purchase and renovation of our headquarters, the Columbia Center. The facility provides affordable meeting and training space for nonprofit organizations.

We hope you will enjoy the recipes from this cookbook for years to come. As we celebrate our 90th anniversary, we pledge to stay true to our mission of training, community service, and improving the quality of life in the Cincinnati and Northern Kentucky areas.

If you would like to learn more about the Junior League of Cincinnati, please visit our Web site at www.jlcincinnati.org.

Thank you for supporting the JLC,

Elizabeth A. Ogle
JLC President 2008–2009

Kate Molinsky
JLC President 2009–2010

Contents

Entrées

92

Side Dishes

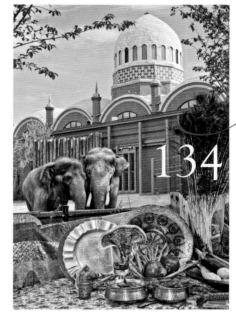

134

Desserts

154

Enclosures

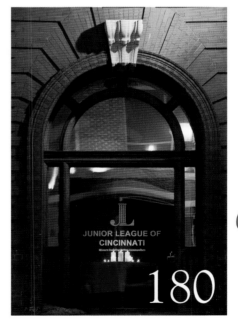

180

Beverages & Appetizers

Great American Ball Park

America's favorite pastime hasn't changed much since the Cincinnati Reds started rounding the bases in 1884, but that doesn't mean local baseball fans haven't enjoyed some improvements along the way.

The hometown team has called five different baseball diamonds home since 1884, starting with League Park. In 1902 Cincinnati baseball fans began cheering the team on at Palace of the Fans, which sat at the intersection of Findlay Street and Western Avenue. The venue featured a unique blend of Roman and Greek styling that was damaged several times by fire. In 1912 the Reds played in a venue called Redland Park, which was finally renamed Crosley Field in 1934. The ballpark was home to Cincinnati's team for decades, until the Reds relocated to Riverfront Stadium in 1970. The Reds shared the facility with the Cincinnati Bengals football team until baseball fans got their own home once again in 2003.

Great American Ball Park on Pete Rose Way is named after Great American Insurance, a Cincinnati-based company and owner of the park's naming rights. The park's north external wall features the classic line, "Rounding Third and Heading for Home," which was first coined by former Reds pitcher and legendary broadcaster Joe Nuxhall. Once inside the ballpark, Reds fans have a variety of features to enjoy. The Pepsi Power Stacks, located at right center field, are reminiscent of the steamboats that once frequented passage on the Ohio River. The stacks flash, give off smoke, and launch fireworks to rally fans or celebrate the Reds' efforts. Crosley Terrace is a nod to Crosley Field and features bronze statues of Crosley-era stars including Nuxhall, Ernie Lombardi, Ted Kluszewski, and Frank Robinson, all posed to look like an imaginary baseball game featuring the Reds' greats.

Baseball fanatics can learn more about the team's legends and lore at the Cincinnati Reds Hall of Fame and Museum, located on the west side of Great American Ball Park. The Hall of Fame and Museum celebrate the Reds' past players and memories through multimedia and memorabilia. You can find more information on Great American Ball Park and Cincinnati's hometown team by visiting www.reds.com.

4th of July Barbecue

Citrus Champagne Punch

———

Parmesan Pesto Bean Dip

Savory Watermelon Salad

———

Summer Corn & Zucchini

Caribbean Spiced Grilled Shrimp

Asparagus Chicken Rollups

———

Savannah Peach Cobbler

Big Apple Bellinis

Serves 4 to 6

*The next time your girlfriends are planning a happy hour,
skip a night out on the town and celebrate in style at home! This cocktail
is best enjoyed with good friends.*

1 (12-ounce) package frozen sliced peaches
8 cups prosecco
1/4 cup orange liqueur
1/4 cup peach schnapps
Mint sprigs for garnish

Combine one-half of the peaches and one-half of the wine in a blender and process until smooth. Remove to a pitcher. Combine the remaining peaches and wine in the blender and process until smooth. Add to the pitcher. Stir in the liqueur and schnapps. Pour into glasses and garnish with mint sprigs.

Champagne Cocktail

Serves 20

1 (46-ounce) can pineapple juice
1 (6-ounce) can frozen limeade concentrate, thawed
2 (750-milliliter) bottles Champagne, chilled

Mix the pineapple juice and limeade concentrate in a punch bowl. Chill until cold. Stir in the Champagne gently and serve.

In 1869 the Cincinnati Red Stockings (a.k.a. the Cincinnati Reds) became the world's first professional (all paid players, no amateurs) baseball team.

Beverages&Appetizers

Frosty Café Cocktails

Serves 2 to 3

*This recipe tastes decadent, but is actually low-fat. It is a perfect
hot weather treat with or without the coffee liqueur.*

1 tablespoon instant espresso powder	1/2 cup fat-free half-and-half
2 tablespoons water	1/3 cup caramel-flavored coffee liqueur
2 large ice cubes	6 to 10 large ice cubes
3 tablespoons caramel	Low-fat whipped cream and shaved
ice cream topping	chocolate for garnish

Combine the espresso powder and water in a microwave-safe cup. Microwave
on High for 45 seconds. Stir until the coffee is dissolved. Add two ice cubes and
stir until the ice is melted. Stir in the caramel topping. Pour into a blender.
Add the half-and-half, liqueur and six to ten ice cubes. Process until thick and
smooth. Pour into glasses. Garnish with low-fat whipped cream and shaved
chocolate and serve immediately.

Lazy-Day Sunday Margaritas

Serves 6

*Whip up this easy cocktail for your family and friends
on game day, a lazy afternoon on the back patio, or for any festive
occasion. The beer gives the margaritas a hint of carbonation
and adds a unique twist on an old favorite.*

1 (12-ounce) can frozen limeade	1/2 cup orange liqueur
concentrate, thawed	1 (12-ounce) can light beer
1 1/2 cups water	1 lime, cut into 6 wedges for garnish
1 1/2 cups tequila	

Mix the limeade concentrate, water, tequila, liqueur and beer in a pitcher.
Pour into glasses filled with ice and garnish each with a lime wedge.

NOTE: *You may substitute lemon-lime soda for the water for added carbonation.
You may also cut back on the tequila if strong drinks don't suit your taste.*

Cincinnati Seasoned

Members of the Junior League of Cincinnati choral group

New Best Friend

Serves 10

This is a strong cocktail that's perfect for serving party guests just getting acquainted with each other. By the end of the evening, your friends will know some people whom they can call new best friends, thanks to your ice-breaking beverage.

2 pound fresh strawberries
1 liter high-quality bourbon
1 cup orange juice

1/2 cup lemon juice
2 tablespoons sugar
10 fresh basil leaves

Remove ten strawberries and set aside for the garnish. Slice the remaining strawberries. Pour the bourbon over one-half of the sliced strawberries in a large bowl and let soak for 8 hours. Remove the strawberries with a slotted spoon to a bowl. Add the remaining strawberries to the bourbon and let soak for 8 hours. Pour through a wire mesh strainer into a pitcher. Purée both batches of soaked strawberries in a blender. Combine the orange juice, lemon juice and sugar in a small pitcher and stir until the sugar is dissolved. Rub one basil leaf around the rim of each of ten tall glasses and shred the basil leaf into the glass. Fill each glass with ice. Fill each glass halfway with the strained bourbon and add a splash of the fruit juice and a splash of the strawberry purée. Garnish each drink with a whole strawberry and serve.

Tart Rum Slush

Serves 8

1 (12-ounce) can frozen limeade concentrate, thawed
1 (12-ounce) can frozen pink lemonade concentrate, thawed
6 cups water

1/2 cup peach schnapps
2 1/2 cups light rum
Club soda, chilled
Fresh mint leaves or maraschino cherries for garnish

Combine the limeade concentrate, lemonade concentrate, water, schnapps and rum in a covered freezer container and mix well. Freeze, covered, until slushy. Spoon into glasses and top each with a splash of club soda. Garnish with a fresh mint leaf or a maraschino cherry.

Tart Whiskey Slush

Serves 6 to 8

1 (12-ounce) can frozen lemonade concentrate, thawed
1 (12-ounce) can frozen orange juice
    concentrate, thawed
1/2 to 3/4 cup pineapple juice
4 cups ginger ale
2 cups whiskey
Lemon-lime soda, chilled
Lemon slices for garnish

Combine the lemonade concentrate, orange juice concentrate, pineapple juice, ginger ale and whiskey in a covered freezer container and mix well. Freeze, covered, until slushy. Spoon into glasses and top each with a splash of lemon-lime soda. Garnish each drink with a lemon slice.

Skip and Go Naked

Serves 12

1 (12-ounce) can frozen lemonade concentrate
1 1/2 cups vodka
Crushed ice
1 (12-ounce) can beer

Combine the lemonade concentrate and vodka in a blender and add crushed ice to fill. Process until slushy. Pour into a pitcher and stir in the beer. For an added splash of flavor, add 1/2 cup cranberry juice cocktail.

The Queen City is a haven for oenophiles, what with the city's annual Cincinnati International Wine Festival. Founded in 1991, the event invites some of the best and most innovative wineries to come to Cincinnati to show off the latest trends in winemaking. The festival also raises money for local charitable organizations and has invested more than $2.75 million in the community since its beginning. Whether you like a sweet riesling, a tannin-filled cabernet, or even a sparkly Champagne, the Cincinnati International Wine Festival at Duke Energy Center has something you'll enjoy sipping.

Sangria Roja o Blanca

Serves 4

1 (750-milliliter) bottle red wine or pinot grigio
1/4 cup sugar
1/4 cup orange liqueur
1/4 cup brandy
1 orange, sliced
1 apple, sliced
1 (12-ounce) can club soda

Combine the wine, sugar, liqueur and brandy in a pitcher and stir until the sugar is dissolved. Stir in the orange and apple. Let stand in the refrigerator for 6 hours. Stir in the club soda. Add ice and serve.

NOTE: *You may substitute blueberries or peaches for the orange and apple.*

Chocolate Raspberry Martini

Serves 4

Impress your friends wih this great-tasting martini!

1 cup high-quality vodka
1 cup pure raspberry acai juice
8 fresh or frozen raspberries
High-quality dark chocolate

Place several ice cubes in each of four martini glasses and fill with cold water. Fill a cocktail shaker one-third full with ice. Add the vodka and juice and shake vigorously. Drain the martini glasses and pour the vodka mixture equally into the chilled glasses. Add two raspberries to each drink and grate chocolate over the top.

Citrus Champagne Punch
Serves 12

1 (12-ounce) can frozen pineapple juice
   concentrate, thawed
1 (12-ounce) can frozen lemonade concentrate, thawed
2 (2-liter) bottles ginger ale, chilled
1 (750-milliliter) bottle Champagne, chilled

Mix the pineapple juice concentrate and lemonade concentrate in a punchbowl. Stir in the ginger ale and Champagne and serve immediately.

NOTE: *You may omit the Champagne if you prefer a nonalcoholic punch.*

Champagne Wine Punch
Serves 20

1 (12-ounce) can frozen pink lemonade
   concentrate, thawed
1 (12-ounce) can frozen limeade
   concentrate, thawed
2 (750-milliliter) bottles Champagne, chilled
1 (750-milliliter) bottle riesling, chilled
1 liter soda water, chilled
1 liter lemon-lime soda, chilled
2 lemons, sliced for garnish

Stir the lemonade concentrate, limeade concentrate, Champagne, wine, soda water and lemon-lime soda in a punch bowl. Serve in punch glasses, each garnished with a lemon slice.

Antioxidant Purple Power Smoothies
Serves 2 to 3

Whip up this "special cocktail" for the kids, but don't tell them it's healthy!

> 1 cup 100% grape juice
> 1 1/2 cups frozen blueberries
> 1 banana
> 6 ounces low-fat blueberry yogurt

Combine the juice, blueberries, banana and yogurt in a blender and process until smooth.

Healthy Tropical Fruit Smoothies
Serves 2 to 3

> 1 cup orange-pineapple-banana juice
> 1 banana
> 1 1/2 cups frozen sliced peaches or tropical fruit mix
> 6 ounces low-fat peach or pineapple yogurt

Process the juice, banana, peaches and yogurt in a blender until smooth.

On game day or a hot summer afternoon, Cincinnatians have long loved a nice, cold glass of beer. The Queen City saw its first beer brewery open in 1812 by Davis Embree. A significant German population immigrated to Cincinnati in the 1840s, and the number of local breweries quickly rose to more than thirty. In 1890 Cincinnati became known as the Beer Capital of the World, with local brewers turning out 1,350,000 barrels of beer annually. Most of the local breweries closed their doors for good during Prohibition, but you can see some of their remnants by wandering the streets of Over-the-Rhine.

Savory Olive Feta Cheesecake

Serves 16

24 (2-inch) sesame or butter crackers
3 tablespoons unsalted butter, softened
12 ounces cream cheese, softened
6 ounces crumbled feta cheese
1/4 cup sour cream
1/2 teaspoon dried marjoram
1/2 teaspoon dried oregano
1/4 teaspoon dried rosemary, crushed
2 eggs
1/4 cup sliced black olives
Additional sliced black olives for garnish

Preheat the oven to 300 degrees. Pulse the crackers in a food processor to make crumbs. Add the butter and pulse to mix well. Press the crumb mixture over the bottom of an 8×8-inch baking pan coated with nonstick cooking spray. Beat the cream cheese, feta cheese, sour cream, marjoram, oregano and rosemary in a mixing bowl at medium speed. Add the eggs one at a time, beating well at low speed after each addition. Stir in 1/4 cup olives. Pour evenly over the crumb mixture and smooth the top with a spatula.

Bake for 45 minutes or until golden brown and a wooden pick inserted in the center comes out clean. Remove to a wire rack to cool for 30 minutes. Chill, covered, overnight or until cold. Cut into 1-inch squares with a knife dipped in hot water after each cut. Cut each square in half diagonally. Arrange on a serving plate and garnish each triangle with one-half of a black olive slice.

The popular Bengal phrase "Who Dey," became popular in 1981 when Bengal fans cheered for their team during their run to Super Bowl XVI. Some fans would do the chant, "Who Dey," and other fans would reply, "Nobody!" The cheer again gained national recognition in their 1988 appearance in Super Bowl XXIII.

Sweet Onion Tart

Serves 6 to 8

1 (1-crust) pie pastry

3 cups thinly sliced white onions

1/4 cup (1/2 stick) unsalted butter

3 garlic cloves, minced

2 teaspoons sugar

1 teaspoon salt

1/2 teaspoon white pepper

1/2 teaspoon grated fresh nutmeg

1/2 cup (2 ounces) finely shredded
 Gruyère cheese

3 tablespoons cornstarch or rice flour

1 cup heavy cream

Preheat the oven to 400 degrees. Fit the pastry into a 9-inch pie plate and flute or pinch the edge of the pastry. Line the pastry with baking parchment and spread dried beans over the bottom. Bake for 12 minutes. Remove to a wire rack and remove the beans and baking parchment. Sauté the onions in the butter in a large skillet over medium heat for 20 minutes or until golden brown. Add the garlic and sugar and sauté for 5 minutes. Stir in the salt, white pepper and nutmeg. Spread the onion mixture over the bottom of the pie crust and sprinkle with the cheese. Mix the cornstarch and cream in the skillet until smooth. Cook until the mixture begins to thicken, stirring constantly. Pour evenly over the onion mixture in the crust. Place the tart on a baking sheet. Bake for 25 minutes or until set and golden brown. Serve warm.

Lobster Quesadillas

Serves 10

2 green bell peppers, chopped

2 red bell peppers, chopped

1 red onion, chopped

1 envelope fajita seasoning mix

1 tablespoon olive oil

12 ounces cooked lobster
 meat, chopped

2 tablespoons chopped cilantro

2 tablespoons chopped chives

10 (10-inch) tortillas

8 ounces sharp Cheddar
 cheese, shredded

8 ounces Monterey Jack
 cheese, shredded

Preheat the oven to 350 degrees. Sauté the bell peppers, onion and seasoning mix in the olive oil in a saucepan over medium heat until the vegetables are tender. Add the lobster, cilantro and chives and sauté for 1 to 2 minutes.

Spoon the lobster mixture over one-half of each tortilla. Sprinkle with the cheeses. Fold the tortillas over the filling and place on a greased baking sheet. Bake for 10 minutes or until the cheese is melted. Cut each tortilla in half and arrange on a serving plate.

Prosciutto and Gruyère Pinwheels
Makes 40 pinwheels

> 1 sheet frozen puff pastry
> 3/4 cup (3 ounces) finely shredded Gruyère cheese
> 4 teaspoons fresh sage
> 1 egg, beaten
> 2 ounces prosciutto

Thaw the puff pastry at room temperature for 30 minutes or until easy to handle. Combine the cheese and sage in a bowl and mix well. Lay the pastry on a lightly floured surface with the short side at the bottom. Cut the pastry in half crosswise. Brush the far long side edge of each pastry half with the egg. Arrange the prosciutto evenly over the pastry halves, avoiding the edge brushed with egg. Spread the cheese mixture evenly over the prosciutto. Roll up each pastry and press the egg-brushed edge to seal. Wrap each pastry roll in waxed paper and chill, seam side down, for up to 3 days. Preheat the oven to 400 degrees. Remove the waxed paper from the pastry rolls and cut into 1/2-inch slices. Place the slices 1 inch apart on a lightly greased baking sheet. Bake for 14 to 16 minutes or until golden brown.

Crème de Pesto
Serves 30

Celebrate some of the best flavors of Italy with this simple recipe. It's very easy to double, and the presentation looks great on any hors d'oeuvre table.

> 8 ounces cream cheese, softened
> 1/4 cup milk
> 30 melba toast crackers
> 1/2 cup plus 2 tablespoons prepared pesto
> 15 oil-pack sun-dried tomatoes, drained and
>   cut in halves

Beat the cream cheese and milk in a mixing bowl until light and fluffy. Spread a layer of the cream cheese mixture over each cracker. Top each with a teaspoon of pesto and then with a sun-dried tomato half. Arrange on a serving plate and chill for 2 hours.

Cincinnati Seasoned

Spinach and Artichoke Bruschetta

Serves 8

1 cup mayonnaise
1 cup (4 ounces) shredded Parmesan cheese
1/4 cup chopped green onions (about 4)
1 (14-ounce) can artichoke hearts, drained and
    coarsely chopped
1 (10-ounce) package frozen chopped spinach, thawed
    and squeezed dry
Salt and pepper to taste
1 baguette, cut into 1/3-inch slices

Preheat the broiler. Mix the mayonnaise and cheese in a bowl. Stir in the green onions and artichokes. Chop the spinach and add to the mayonnaise mixture. Season with salt and pepper and mix well. Spread equal portions of the spinach mixture over the bread slices. Place the bruschetta in a single layer on a baking sheet. Broil for 2 minutes or until bubbly and light brown.

Hearts of Palm Amuse-Bouche

Serves 8 to 12

*A simple, tasty recipe to offer your dinner guests at the
start of a multicourse meal.*

1 (4-ounce) package sliced prosciutto
1 (14-ounce) can hearts of palm, drained

Wrap a slice of prosciutto around each heart of palm. Slice into 3/4-inch pieces and serve.

NOTE: *You may also drizzle balsamic vinegar over the appetizer once it's arranged on the plate to give it some added punch. Sprinkle with chopped fresh parsley for extra color, if desired. These little bites also make a great salad garnish.*

Miniature Goat Cheese Sweet Peppers

Serves 30

30 red, yellow and/or orange miniature sweet peppers
18 ounces semi-soft goat cheese (chèvre)
1/4 cup chopped fresh chives, tarragon, basil or thyme
Fresh basil for garnish

Preheat the oven to 350 degrees. Cut a slit from the top to the bottom of each pepper, leaving the stem intact. Remove the seeds from the peppers using a small spoon. Combine the cheese and chives in a bowl and mix well. Spoon into a pastry bag. Pipe the cheese mixture into each pepper. Arrange the stuffed peppers close together on a nonstick baking sheet. Bake for 8 to 10 minutes or until the cheese is heated through and the peppers are tender-crisp. Remove to a serving plate and garnish with fresh basil.

Smoked Salmon Pinwheels

Serves 12

8 ounces cream cheese, softened
2 teaspoons horseradish
1 pound smoked salmon
Lettuce leaves
Lemon wedges for garnish
Capers for garnish

Combine the cream cheese and horseradish in a bowl and mix well. Spread a thin layer of the cream cheese mixture over slices of smoked salmon and roll up. Cut into bite-size slices. Serve on a lettuce-lined platter and garnish with lemon wedges and capers.

Athenian Hummus
Serves 8

1 (15-ounce) can garbanzo beans
1 garlic clove
1 tablespoon fresh lemon juice
Dash of salt
1 teaspoon extra-virgin olive oil
1¹/2 teaspoons fresh rosemary
2 ounces feta cheese, crumbled
Dash of paprika

Drain one-half of the liquid from the beans and discard. Process the beans, remaining liquid and garlic in a blender for 1 minute. Add the lemon juice, salt, olive oil and rosemary slowly, processing constantly until smooth. Remove to a serving bowl and chill for 1 to 2 hours. Sprinkle with the feta cheese and paprika. Serve with vegetables, chips and/or bread.

NOTE: *This is a great dish with a lot of flavor, and can be a healthy option if you choose to use all organic ingredients. It's quick and easy to make when you have last-minute guests.*

Greek Cheese Ball
Serves 10 to 15

16 ounces cream cheese, softened
2 small cans chopped black olives, drained
1/2 cup minced red onion
3/4 cup feta cheese
4 slices bacon, crisp-cooked and crumbled
1/2 cup chopped walnuts

Combine the cream cheese, olives, onion, feta cheese and bacon in a bowl and mix well with your hands. Form into a ball and place on a serving plate. Pat the walnuts onto the cheese ball. Chill for 4 hours or overnight. Serve with crispy wheat crackers.

Cincinnati Seasoned

Sicilian Cheese Ball

Serves 10 to 15

4 ounces prosciutto
16 ounces cream cheese, softened
1 teaspoon Worcestershire sauce
1/2 cup (2 ounces) shredded provolone cheese
2 tablespoons chopped fresh chives
2 teaspoons dried oregano

Remove five to six pieces of prosciutto and set aside. Chop the remaining proscuitto. Combine the chopped prosciutto, cream cheese, Worcestershire sauce and provolone cheese in a bowl and mix well. Form into a ball. Mix the chives and oregano on a piece of waxed paper. Roll the cheese ball in the herbs to coat. Wrap the reserved prosciutto slices around the cheese ball. Serve with assorted crackers.

NOTE: *You may make two smaller cheese balls instead of one large one, if desired.*

Caramel Brie Dip

Serves 8

This is a simple recipe you can pull together if you're short on time and striving to serve a crowd-pleaser.

1 (5-inch) round Brie cheese
3 tablespoons caramel apple dip, warmed
Finely chopped assorted dried fruits, such as cranberries,
    apricots, pineapple and apples
Finely chopped nuts, such as walnuts and pecans

Preheat the oven to 350 degrees. Place the cheese in a small baking pan. Bake for 15 minutes. Remove the cheese to a serving plate and drizzle with the warm caramel dip. Sprinkle the fruits and nuts over the top and serve with assorted crackers.

Sweet Harvest Brie
Serves 8

Brie is a perfect addition to any party spread, and this recipe is especially perfect for bringing out the flavors of autumn.

1 (8-ounce) round Brie cheese
1 Granny Smith apple, chopped
1/4 cup pine nuts
1/4 cup packed brown sugar

Preheat the oven to 350 degrees. Place the cheese in a small baking pan. Top with the apple, pine nuts and brown sugar. Bake for 20 minutes. Serve with baguette slices.

Brie with Wine Glaze
Serves 8

Serve this beautiful appetizer at a cocktail party or spring get-together. It's simple to make, but the presentation really wows the crowd!

1 envelope unflavored gelatin
1 cup Champagne
1 (8-ounce) round Brie cheese
4 or 5 strawberries, thinly sliced vertically
1 mint sprig, or mint leaves

Sprinkle the gelatin over the Champagne in a small saucepan. Stir gently a few times and let stand for 5 minutes to soften. Cook over low heat until the gelatin is dissolved, stirring occasionally. Place the saucepan in a bowl of ice water and stir the gelatin mixture until thick. Place the cheese on a serving plate. Brush the entire surface of the cheese with the wine glaze. Arrange the strawberry slices and mint sprig or mint leaves in a decorative pattern over the top of the cheese. Brush the strawberries and mint with the glaze until completely covered. Chill until ready to serve.

NOTE: *Refrigerate any leftovers or the glaze will soften and drip off the top of the cheese.*

Cincinnati Seasoned

Mock Crab Sandwich Spread

Serves 24

1 white onion, chopped
3 tablespoons milk
4 ounces white Cheddar
    cheese, shredded

8 ounces fresh tomatoes, peeled,
    cored and chopped
1 egg, beaten

Sauté the onion in the milk in a saucepan until tender. Stir in the cheese and tomatoes. Cook until the cheese is melted, stirring constantly with a wooden spoon. Remove from the heat and stir in the egg gradually. Return to the heat and cook until the mixture begins to thicken, stirring constantly. Remove to a bowl and let cool. Chill until cold. Spread over crackers or baguette slices.

NOTE: *Use this spread within twenty-four hours of making it.*

Hot Crab and Artichoke Dip

Serves 16

3 garlic cloves, minced
1 shallot, minced
1 tablespoon olive oil
1 cup sour cream
1 cup (4 ounces) Italian
    six-cheese blend
8 ounces cream cheese, softened
1/4 cup dry sherry
1 tablespoon confectioners' sugar
Juice of 1 lemon

1 teaspoon dry mustard
Dash of Worcestershire sauce
1 1/2 teaspoons Tabasco sauce
3 tablespoons Old Bay seasoning
Salt to taste
1 (14-ounce) can artichoke
    hearts, drained
1 pound crab meat, shells removed
    and meat flaked
1/4 cup shredded Romano cheese

Preheat the oven to 350 degrees. Sauté the garlic and shallot in the olive oil in a skillet until tender. Remove to a bowl. Add the sour cream, six-cheese blend, cream cheese, wine, confectioners' sugar, lemon juice, dry mustard, Worcestershire sauce, Tabasco sauce, Old Bay seasoning and salt and mix well. Fold in the artichokes and crab meat. Spoon into a baking dish and sprinkle with the Romano cheese. Bake for 40 minutes or until bubbly and golden brown. Serve with crostini, baguette slices or crackers.

Artichoke Dip with Capers

Serves 4 to 6

2 cups mayonnaise

2 cups (8 ounces) grated
    Parmesan cheese

1 (28-ounce) can water-pack
    artichoke hearts, drained

3 strips roasted red peppers, chopped

4 teaspoons rinsed drained capers

1/4 cup (1 ounce) grated
    Parmesan cheese

Preheat the oven to 400 degrees. Mix the mayonnaise, 2 cups cheese, the artichokes, roasted peppers and capers in a bowl. Spoon into a greased 9×9-inch baking pan. Sprinkle with 1/4 cup cheese. Bake for 15 minutes or until golden brown and bubbling.

World's Best Spinach and Artichoke Dip

Serves 20

1 (10-ounce) package frozen spinach,
    thawed and drained

1 (14-ounce) package frozen
    artichoke hearts

1 small onion, minced

3 garlic cloves, minced

16 ounces light cream cheese

1/2 teaspoon oregano

1/2 teaspoon red pepper flakes

1 tablespoon lemon juice

1/3 cup grated Parmesan cheese

Salt and pepper to taste

Minced red bell pepper or chopped
    tomato for garnish

Chop the spinach in a food processor. Add the artichokes and pulse until chunky. Coat a medium saucepan with nonstick cooking spray. Add the onion and garlic and sauté over medium heat for 5 minutes or until translucent. Stir in the artichoke mixture, cream cheese, oregano, red pepper flakes and lemon juice. Cook until bubbly, stirring frequently. Stir in the Parmesan cheese, salt and pepper. Garnish with bell pepper or tomato and serve immediately with vegetables or baked chips.

NOTE: *Don't worry about getting the spinach completely dry—the extra moisture will help to thin the dip.*

This recipe is from
Cincinnati-based
www.sparkrecipes.com.

Hot Bacon Dip

Serves 8 to 12

8 ounces cream cheese, softened
8 ounces cheese, shredded
1/2 cup mayonnaise
3 green onions, chopped
1/4 cup finely chopped Vidalia onion
12 slices bacon, crisp-cooked and crumbled

Preheat the oven to 375 degrees. Mix the cream cheese and shredded cheese in a bowl. Combine the mayonnaise, green onions, Vidalia onion and one-half of the bacon in a bowl. Add to the cheese mixture and mix well. Spoon into a 9×9-inch baking dish and sprinkle with the remaining bacon. Bake for 20 minutes. Serve with corn chips, garlic chips or tortilla chips.

Chunky Guacamole

Serves 4

2 avocados
1 tomato, chopped
1 teaspoon minced fresh garlic
1 tablespoon fresh lime juice
1/2 teaspoon sea salt
1/2 teaspoon pepper
1/4 cup chopped cilantro for garnish

Cut the avocados in half and remove the seed. Cut a criss-cross pattern in the avocados with a knife. Scoop out the avocado chunks into a bowl using a spoon. Add the tomato, garlic, lime juice, salt and pepper and mix gently. Garnish with the cilantro and serve.

NOTE: *Make sure your avocados are ripe. You can add onions for some extra zip. If you like heat in your guacamole, add a teaspoon of chili powder and a dash of Tabasco sauce.*

The CANDO program links groups of JLC volunteers with community organizations for a variety of high-impact "done-in-a-day" projects.

Layered Greek Dip

Serves 16

8 ounces cream cheese, softened

1 tablespoon fresh lemon juice

1 teaspoon dried Italian seasoning

2 or 3 garlic cloves, minced

1 1/2 cups prepared hummus

1 cup chopped unpeeled cucumber

1 cup chopped cherry tomatoes

1/2 cup chopped pitted kalamata olives

1/2 cup crumbled feta cheese

1/3 cup sliced green onions

Beat the cream cheese, lemon juice, Italian seasoning and garlic in a mixing bowl until fluffy. Spread over the bottom of a shallow serving dish. Spread the hummus evenly over the cream cheese mixture. Layer the cucumber, tomatoes, olives, feta cheese and green onions over the hummus in the order listed. Chill, covered, for 2 to 4 hours. Serve with pita chips.

NOTE: *Feel free to use one-third-less-fat cream cheese if you are striving to make this recipe more healthful.*

Tyrokafteri (Spicy Feta Dip)

Serves 4

Mediterranean cooking is constantly evolving, and it's a great style of food that allows experimentation with different methods. This particular dip gives you the "kick" to make a dish pop, and the feta offers a nice, rich, and salted balance to make it all come together.

16 ounces crumbled feta cheese

1 red bell pepper

2 tablespoons cayenne pepper

1 tablespoon basil or oregano

1 tablespoon grated lemon zest

Juice of 1 lemon

1/2 cup extra-virgin olive oil

Process the cheese, bell pepper, cayenne pepper, basil and lemon zest in a food processor. Add the lemon juice and olive oil gradually, processing constantly until smooth and creamy. Remove to a serving bowl and surround with pita wedges, crackers and/or pretzels.

Tailgate!

Lazy-Day Sunday Margaritas

Reuben Dip

Athenian Hummus

Autumn Chicken Salad

Hot Crab & Artichoke Dip

Oatmeal Chocolate Bars

Soft & Moist Pumpkin Cookies

Paul Brown Stadium

If you are ever wandering along the Cincinnati riverfront and looking for an exiting, entertaining option to fill your day, you only need to follow the orange-and-black striped crowd to soak in a Queen City tradition.

Paul Brown Stadium sits along the riverfront, waiting to erupt with excitement each autumn. The Cincinnati Bengals football team began playing in the Stadium in 2000 after years of sharing Riverfront Stadium/Cinergy Field with the Cincinnati Reds. Today, every game day brings up to 67,000 fans to the sprawling facility on 22 acres.

The Stadium features an innovative design and futuristic look which, from above, resembles the shape of a horseshoe. This shape, often seen as a good luck charm, did not happen by chance. Planners designed the space so as to prevent having "bad seats." Seventy percent of fans are seated on the sidelines in three tiers, and many are concentrated at the fifty-yard line. The Stadium won a Business Week/Architectural record design award in 2002. Some lucky spectators also have the opportunity to enjoy one of the 114 private suites and 2 clubs with sweeping views of both the Ohio River and Downtown Cincinnati.

Winning or losing, Cincinnatians are die-hard fans who pack the house every home game. When the Bengals are in town, roaring fans prowl into Paul Brown Stadium with the sound of Guns N' Roses' "Welcome to the Jungle," blaring from its speakers.

You can learn more about Paul Brown Stadium and the Cincinnati Bengals by visiting www.bengals.com.

Parmesan Pesto Bean Dip

Serves 4

*This is a low-calorie, healthy option to serve when the gang's
over to watch the ballgame.*

1 (15-ounce) can cannellini beans
3 tablespoons pine nuts
3 tablespoons shredded Parmesan cheese
3 tablespoons extra-virgin olive oil
15 to 20 fresh basil leaves, shredded
1/4 teaspoon coarse sea salt
Freshly ground pepper to taste

Drain three-fourths of the liquid from the beans and discard. Pour the
remaining liquid and beans into a blender or food processor. Add the pine nuts,
cheese, olive oil, basil, salt and pepper and process until creamy.

NOTE: *Olive oil is great for your heart, while the cannellini beans are full of fiber.
The basil, pine nuts, and Parmesan cheese give this dip some fantastic flavor.*

Pepperoni Pizza Dip

Serves 8 to 10

8 ounces cream cheese, softened
1/2 cup canned pizza sauce
1 onion, chopped
1 (4-ounce) can chopped black olives, drained
2 cups (8 ounces) shredded mozzarella cheese
1 (6-ounce) package sliced pepperoni, chopped

Preheat the oven to 350 degrees. Spread the cream cheese over the bottom of
a shallow baking dish. Layer the pizza sauce, onion, olives, mozzarella cheese and
pepperoni over the cream cheese in the order listed. Bake for 30 minutes or until
the edges are bubbly. Serve with scoop-style corn chips.

*The Cincinnati Bengals
football club was
formed in 1937 as a
member of the American
Football League.*

Reuben Dip

Serves 12

A unique dip that offers all the flavors of your favorite deli sandwich!
Make sure you serve it to your hungry crowd while it's still hot.

2 (6-ounce) packages corned beef,
    cut into 1/2-inch pieces
1/2 cup chili sauce
3/4 cup Thousand Island salad dressing
8 ounces Swiss cheese, shredded
1 (8-ounce) can sauerkraut, rinsed and drained

Preheat the oven to 350 degrees. Combine the corned beef, chili sauce, salad dressing, cheese and sauerkraut in a bowl and mix well. Spoon into a shallow baking dish. Bake for 30 minutes. Serve with melba toast crackers.

Caprese Salsa

Serves 6 to 8

Dish up a fun variation on an Italian classic.

8 fresh basil leaves
2 cups red grape tomatoes, cut into quarters
2 yellow tomatoes, cut into 1/2-inch pieces
8 ounces fresh mozzarella cheese, cut into 1/2-inch pieces
Sea salt and crushed pepper to taste
2 garlic cloves, minced
1/2 cup extra-virgin olive oil
1 baguette, cut into 1/2-inch slices
1/2 cup extra-virgin olive oil

Preheat the oven to 350 degrees. Stack the basil leaves together and roll up tightly. Slice with a knife or kitchen shears. Combine the basil, grape tomatoes, yellow tomatoes, cheese, salt, pepper and garlic in a bowl. Drizzle with 1/2 cup olive oil and toss gently to combine. Remove to a serving bowl. Place the bread slices on a baking sheet and drizzle with 1/2 cup olive oil. Bake for 10 minutes or until toasted. Dip the bread into the salsa or spoon the salsa onto the bread to serve.

Garden Fresh Salsa

Serves 10 to 12

This salsa is tomato-free and is a delicious addition to any summer dinner either as an appetizer or served over a green salad.

1 (15-ounce) can black beans, rinsed
    and well drained
1 (12-ounce) can Shoe Peg corn,
    well drained
1 red bell pepper, finely chopped
1 yellow bell pepper, finely chopped
1 orange bell pepper, finely chopped

1 large red onion, finely chopped
3/4 cup vinegar
3/4 cup vegetable oil
1 cup sugar
5 tablespoons Tiger sauce
Salt and pepper to taste

Combine the beans, corn, bell peppers and onion in a bowl and toss to mix. Whisk the vinegar, oil, sugar and hot sauce in a bowl. Pour over the vegetables and mix well. Chill, covered, overnight. Drain, reserving the marinade. Sprinkle the salsa with salt and pepper and serve with tortilla chips. Store any leftovers in the reserved marinade in the refrigerator.

Mango–Pineapple Salsa

Makes 3 cups

1/2 red onion, chopped
1/2 red bell pepper, chopped
1/2 orange bell pepper, chopped
1/4 cup chopped fresh cilantro
1/4 cup chopped fresh parsley
1 tablespoon minced fresh garlic

1 cup chopped fresh pineapple
1 mango, cut into small pieces
1 jalapeño chile, chopped
1 tablespoon southwest chipotle
    seasoning blend
Juice of 1 lime

Combine the onion, bell peppers, cilantro, parsley, garlic, pineapple, mango and jalapeño chile in a bowl and toss to mix. Add the seasoning blend and lime juice and toss to coat. Chill until cold. Serve with tortilla chips.

Saigon Salsa

Serves 8 to 10

8 or 9 large Roma tomatoes, chopped
1 red onion, chopped
$^1/_4$ cup (or more) finely
    chopped cilantro
Juice of 2 limes

1 teaspoon salt
1 teaspoon sugar
3 or 4 Thai chiles, finely
    chopped (optional)

Combine eight tomatoes, the onion and cilantro in a bowl and mix well. Add cilantro if there is more red than green, or add another chopped tomato if more red is need to balance the color. Add the lime juice, salt, sugar and chiles and mix well. Chill for 1 hour. Stir and serve with tortilla chips.

NOTE: *If you do not like heat, do not add the chiles. If you like a really hot salsa, add eight to ten chiles.*

Santa Fe Salsa

Serves 16

If you're looking for the perfect topping for salad greens or a grilled chicken breast, this salsa is it! You can also serve it as a dip.

2 (15-ounce) cans black beans,
    rinsed and drained
1 (12-ounce) can white corn,
    rinsed and drained
2 tomatoes, seeded and chopped
1 cup chopped celery

3 garlic cloves, minced
1 green bell pepper, chopped
$^1/_2$ cup chopped fresh parsley
2 tablespoons chopped cilantro
1 (4-ounce) jar diced pimentos
$^3/_4$ cup Italian salad dressing

Combine the beans, corn, tomatoes, celery, garlic, bell pepper, parsley, cilantro and pimentos in a bowl and mix well. Add the salad dressing and toss lightly to coat. Chill for 8 to 10 hours, stirring occasionally. Serve with tortilla chips.

Breakfast, Breads & Brunch

Roebling Bridge

By the mid-1800s, Cincinnati had become the nation's leading inland ferry and port destination, and it became evident that a bridge was needed spanning the grand Ohio River to Kentucky. Designing the bridge presented quite a challenge, but German engineer John A. Roebling was just the man for the task. Construction started in September 1856, but by 1858 work was halted due to lack of funding and the Civil War. Later, a renewed interest in the bridge and funds from the selling of stock allowed for the construction to start again with John A. Roebling returning to continue the work.

Open to traffic on January 1, 1867, and originally called the "Covington-Cincinnati Suspension Bridge," it was the first span to use both vertical suspenders and diagonal stays fanning from each of its 230-foot stone towers. Travelers had to pay a toll to cross the bridge: the driver of a horse and buggy, $0.15; three horses and a carriage, $0.25;

pedestrians, $0.01. The bridge was the longest in the world at the time, spanning 1,057 feet across the Ohio River between Covington and Cincinnati. The bridge held on to that status until 1883, when Roebling's Brooklyn Bridge was completed.

The structure has undergone some changes over time, including receiving a second set of main cables and a wider steel deck in 1896. In 1953 the Covington-Cincinnati Bridge Company sold the bridge to the Commonwealth of Kentucky for $4.2 million. In 1975 the bridge was listed on the National Register of Historic places, and in 1983 it was designated a National Historic Civil Engineering landmark and was renamed after Roebling. Having stood the test of time, the John A. Roebling Bridge has become one of the most recognizable symbols of Cincinnati. Learn more at www.roeblingbridge.com

New Year's Day Brunch

Big Apple Bellinis

Zucchini with Dilled Cream Sauce

Sour Cream Coffee Cake

Artichoke Squares

Bacon Quiche Breakfast Cups

Spicy Shrimp & Creamy Grits

Hot Chocolate Mousse

Baked Spinach Tomato Frittata

Serves 4

2 potatoes, peeled

2 tablespoons olive oil

1 tablespoon unsalted butter

1/4 cup thinly sliced onion

Kosher salt and freshly ground pepper
    to taste

6 eggs, beaten

1 (10-ounce) package frozen
    chopped spinach, thawed and
    squeezed dry

2 small ripe red tomatoes, sliced

3/4 cup (3 ounces) shredded Swiss
    cheese or mozzarella cheese

Preheat the oven to 350 degrees. Cut the potatoes into halves and slice 1/8 inch thick. Cook the potatoes in the olive oil and butter in a large skillet over medium heat until tender and light brown, turning as needed. Add the onion and sauté for 2 to 3 minutes. Spread the potato mixture in a nonstick 9×9-inch baking pan. Season with salt and pepper. Pour the eggs over the potatoes. Top with the spinach; layer the tomatoes over the top. Sprinkle with the cheese. Bake for 20 minutes or until set. Cut into four squares and serve hot.

NOTE: *The frittata can be served at room temperature as an appetizer.*

Miniature Vegetable Frittatas

Makes 9 frittatas

5 eggs

2 tablespoons low-fat milk

2 ounces goat cheese, crumbled

1 cup chopped tomato

2 cups chopped fresh or thawed
    frozen broccoli

Salt and pepper to taste

Salsa (optional)

Preheat the oven to 350 degrees. Whisk the eggs and milk in a bowl. Stir in the cheese, tomato, broccoli, salt and pepper. Spoon into muffin cups coated with nonstick cooking spray. Bake for 15 minutes or until set and golden brown. Top with salsa and add toast for a complete breakfast.

NOTE: *These can be made in advance and chilled. Reheat in the microwave.*

This recipe is from
Cincinnati-based
www.sparkrecipes.com.

Christmas Morning Italian Strata
Serves 12

*This is a wonderful dish for Christmas morning or any morning
when you may be entertaining houseguests.*

1 1/2 pounds Italian sausage, casings removed
1 (12-ounce) loaf French bread, cut into 1/2-inch pieces
8 ounces fresh or drained canned mushrooms
1/2 cup chopped green bell pepper (optional)
1 (10-ounce) package frozen chopped spinach, thawed
    and squeezed dry (optional)
6 eggs
4 cups milk
2 teaspoons Italian seasoning
1/2 teaspoon garlic powder
1/4 teaspoon pepper
8 ounces mozzarella cheese, shredded
4 ounces Cheddar cheese, shredded
1/4 cup chopped parsley for garnish

Brown the sausage in a skillet, stirring until crumbly; drain. Layer the sausage, bread, mushrooms, bell peppers and spinach in a greased 9×13-inch baking dish. Whisk the eggs, milk, Italian seasoning, garlic powder and pepper in a bowl. Pour evenly over the layers in the baking dish. Cover with plastic wrap and chill overnight. Preheat the oven to 350 degrees. Bake the strata, uncovered, for 1 hour. Sprinkle with the mozzarella cheese and Cheddar cheese. Bake for 15 minutes longer or until a knife inserted in the center comes out clean. Remove to a wire rack and garnish with the parsley. Let stand for 10 minutes before serving.

Cincinnati Seasoned

Bacon Quiche Biscuit Cups

Makes 20

4 ounces cream cheese, softened

3 tablespoons milk

4 eggs, beaten

3/4 cup (3 ounces) shredded Cheddar
cheese or Swiss cheese

2 tablespoons chopped green onions

2 (10-count) cans buttermilk biscuits

6 slices bacon, crisp-cooked and
crumbled

Preheat the oven to 350 degrees. Beat the cream cheese, milk and eggs in a mixing bowl until smooth. Stir in the cheese and one-half of the green onions. Separate each can of biscuit dough into ten biscuits. Press one biscuit into the bottom and up the sides of each of twenty well-greased muffin cups. Sprinkle one-half of the crumbled bacon over the biscuits. Fill the muffin cups three-fourths full with the egg mixture. Sprinkle with the remaining bacon and green onions. Bake for 10 minutes or until golden brown.

NOTE: *These may be made one day in advance and chilled. Reheat before serving. They also travel well for a "take along" breakfast or for tailgating.*

Artichoke Squares

Serves 4 to 6

Easy yet elegant finger food, these are perfect for brunch, bridal or baby showers, or as an appetizer. The basil, artichokes, and Parmesan provide a wonderful blend of flavor while the jalapeño offers added kick.

1 (12-ounce) jar marinated artichoke
hearts, drained and chopped

1 red onion, chopped

4 eggs, beaten

1/4 cup fine bread crumbs

Handful of fresh basil, chopped

2 garlic cloves, pressed

2 cups (8 ounces) shredded
Parmesan cheese

1 jalapeño chile, finely chopped

Preheat the oven to 325 degrees. Combine the artichokes, onion, eggs, bread crumbs, basil, garlic, cheese and jalapeño chile in a bowl and mix well. Spread in an 8×8-inch baking pan coated with nonstick cooking spray. Bake for 40 minutes. Let stand for 5 minutes before cutting into squares.

Chicken and Waffle Sandwiches

Serves 3

1 cup mayonnaise
1/2 cup finely chopped chipotle chiles
6 frozen cinnamon waffles, thawed
18 slices smoked chicken breast
3 slices Havarti cheese

Preheat the broiler. Combine the mayonnaise and chiles in a bowl and mix well. Spread 1 tablespoon (or more) of the mayonnaise mixture over three of the waffles and top each with six slices of chicken. Add one slice of the cheese over the chicken and top with the remaining waffles to make three sandwiches. Chill any remaining mayonnaise for another use.

Place the waffle sandwiches on a baking sheet. Broil for 1 minute per side or until the waffles are toasted and the cheese is slightly melted. You may use a toaster oven instead of a broiler, if desired.

This recipe is from
Chef Caitlyn MacEachen Steininger
of "Cooking with Caitlyn."

Cincinnatians love to dine out, and there is no better place to taste and savor the flavors of the city than Taste of Cincinnati. The annual, three-day festival in May showcases bite-size tastes of the best-loved dishes in the region. Whether you love goetta or crepes, you are sure to discover something that tantalizes your taste buds. Taste of Cincinnati not only features the best restaurants and dishes of Greater Cincinnati, but also showcases a variety of bands that are sure to appeal to your musical palate.

Cincinnati Seasoned

Breakfast Burritos

Serves 4

6 eggs, beaten

1 tablespoon milk

1 onion, chopped

1 jalapeño chile, chopped

1 chicken breast, grilled and chopped

1/2 cup (2 ounces) shredded
    Cheddar cheese

4 (10-inch) flour or corn tortillas

1 avocado, sliced

1 cup salsa

Beat the eggs and milk in a bowl. Sauté the onion and jalapeño chile in a nonstick skillet over low heat until tender. Increase the heat to medium and add the eggs. Cook until scrambled, stirring frequently. Stir in the chicken and cheese and cook until heated through. Cover the tortillas with a damp paper towel. Microwave on High for 15 seconds. Spoon one-fourth of the egg mixture onto the center of each tortilla. Top each with one-fourth of the avocado and salsa. Roll up or fold the opposite sides of the tortilla over the center and serve.

NOTE: *Try using cooked turkey sausage or cooked ground chicken instead of grilled chicken. Add chopped cilantro, sour cream, or other burrito toppings for a different flavor and appearance.*

Dutch Baby Pancake

Serves 8

5 1/3 tablespoons butter

4 eggs

1 cup milk

1 cup all-purpose flour

Salt to taste

Maple syrup

Preheat the oven to 425 degrees. Melt the butter in a 3- or 4-quart shallow baking dish or soufflé dish in the oven. Maintain the oven temperature. Process the eggs in a blender at high speed for 1 minute. Add the milk and process to mix. Add the flour and salt slowly, processing constantly for 30 seconds. Pour the batter slowly into the hot baking dish. Bake for 20 minutes or until puffy and golden brown. Drizzle with maple syrup and serve immediately.

NOTE: *You may also make this in a 12-inch ovenproof skillet. Top the pancake with seasonal berries and confectioners' sugar for a flavor twist.*

Mrs. Derrick Vail dictating at Clovernook

Croque Madame
(Nutella and Marshmallow Fluff)

Serves 2

4 slices white bread
Nutella hazelnut spread
Marshmallow fluff
3 eggs

Spread two of the bread slices generously with Nutella. Spread the remaining two bread slices generously with marshmallow fluff and place over the Nutella-covered slices to make two sandwiches. Whisk the eggs in a shallow bowl. Heat a nonstick skillet over high heat. Dip each sandwich in the eggs to coat, scraping off any excess. Fry the sandwiches in the skillet until crispy and golden brown on both sides.

NOTE: *For an extra-special treat, you may also serve this with a spoonful of whipped cream or ice cream.*

This recipe is from
Chef Caitlyn MacEachen Steininger
of "Cooking with Caitlyn."

Kids in the Kitchen began in 2006 and engages kids in the preparation of healthy meals as well as educates them and their parents on healthy meal choices. Junior Leagues in more than 255 locations provide lessons and demonstrations related to the preparation of healthy meals and snacks in partnership with local community organizations, chefs, and nutritionists.

French Toast Casserole

Serves 8 to 10

An incredibly easy dish that is perfect for brunch, especially if you're searching for a recipe you can prepare the night before.

1 (16-ounce) loaf French bread, cut into 1-inch slices
8 eggs
2 cups half-and-half
1 cup 2% milk or whole milk
2 tablespoons granulated sugar
1 teaspoon light brown sugar
1/2 teaspoon cinnamon
1/4 teaspoon nutmeg
1 teaspoon vanilla extract
Dash of salt

1 cup (2 sticks) unsalted butter, melted
1 cup packed light brown sugar
1 cup chopped pecans
1/2 cup chopped almonds
2 tablespoons light corn syrup
1/2 teaspoon cinnamon
1/2 teaspoon nutmeg
2 cups confectioners' sugar
1/4 cup 2% milk or whole milk

Arrange the bread slices in two overlapping rows in a generously buttered 9×13-inch baking dish. Whisk the eggs, half-and-half, 1 cup milk, the granulated sugar, 1 teaspoon brown sugar, 1/2 teaspoon cinnamon, 1/4 teaspoon nutmeg, the vanilla and salt in a bowl. Pour evenly over the bread slices. Cover with foil and chill overnight.

Preheat the oven to 350 degrees. Combine the butter, 1 cup brown sugar, the pecans, almonds, corn syrup, 1/2 teaspoon cinnamon and 1/2 teaspoon nutmeg in a bowl and mix well. Sprinkle evenly over the soaked bread. Bake for 40 minutes or until puffed and golden brown. Whisk the confectioners' sugar and 1/4 cup milk in a bowl until smooth. Drizzle over the casserole. Serve with maple syrup on the side.

NOTE: *If you enjoy bananas, slice two or three bananas and arrange them over the bread before adding the pecan topping and baking.*

Popular in the greater Cincinnati area, goetta is peasant food of German origin brought to the region by immigrants in the nineteenth century. Traditionally a breakfast food, the delicacy was meant to increase the servings of meat over many meals as a way to save money. Goetta is based around ground meat, usually pork, combined with cooked pin-head or other steel-cut oats, flavored with bay leaves, aromatic herbs, salt, and pepper. Typically formed into small loaves, it is cut, fried in meat drippings or bacon drippings, and served with maple syrup, jelly, or ketchup alongside other breakfast items. Also known as "Cincinnati Caviar," goetta has become such a popular side dish that there are entire celebrations dedicated to it.

54

Grape Truffles

Serves 12

Serve this recipe for brunch or as an appetizer. The colors of the grapes and pistachios can make a fun show of color for your holiday gathering.

1 bunch seedless grapes
5 ounces goat cheese
1/4 cup dried cranberries, chopped
1/2 teaspoon cinnamon
8 ounces pistachios, ground

Cut the grapes in half to make them bite-size if necessary. Combine the cheese, cranberries and cinnamon in a bowl and mix well. Cover each grape with a small amount of the cheese mixture and roll into a ball. Coat in the ground pistachios.

Greek Yogurt Parfait

Serves 6

A simple recipe that is excellent for breakfast, brunch, or even dessert.

24 ounces plain Greek yogurt
1/4 teaspoon almond extract
2 teaspoons honey
Thinly sliced melon
Granola

Mix the yogurt and almond extract in a bowl. Spoon 1/4 cup of the yogurt into each of six large wine glasses. Drizzle evenly with 1 teaspoon of the honey and top each with a melon slice. Repeat the layers to use the remaining yogurt, honey and melon. Top with granola. Serve chilled.

Wiedemann Hill Mansion

The historic Wiedemann Hill Mansion stands majestically above the city of Newport, Kentucky, with breathtaking views of Cincinnati and the surrounding area.

Charles Wiedemann, heir to the George Wiedemann Brewery, built the Mansion in 1894. The noted architect Samuel Hannaford (Cincinnati Music Hall, Cincinnati City Hall, The Cincinnatian Hotel, The Wiedemann Brewery) designed the magnificent chateauesque-style mansion.

The original grounds spread over twelve acres and included formal gardens, a swimming pool, greenhouse, carriage house, and vineyards. The seventeen-room house includes seven bathrooms, two half-baths, and a magnificent custom-built Rookwood fireplace depicting a Bavarian castle. The reception rooms are adorned in many different types of wood and include antique handpainted tin ceilings.

The home remained in the Weidemann family until 1951, when the Diocese of Covington purchased the property for Bishop William Mulloy. Several acres were subsequently parceled off, among them the footprint for Newport Central Catholic High School.

Current owners Donna and Roger Weddle began a two-year restoration project in 2005, meticulously restoring every detail in the Mansion to its former splendor, including some modern amenities such as air conditioning, an elevator, and a stunning professional kitchen.

This historical gem is now the setting for many events including weddings, rehearsal dinners, corporate functions, cocktail parties, and corporate retreats. Discover the Mansion by visiting www.whillmansion.com.

Sour Cream Coffee Cake

Serves 10 to 12

2 cups all-purpose flour
1 teaspoon baking powder
1 teaspoon baking soda
1/2 teaspoon salt
1 cup (2 sticks) margarine, softened
1 cup granulated sugar
2 eggs
1 cup sour cream
1 teaspoon vanilla extract
1 cup packed brown sugar
1/2 cup granulated sugar
2 teaspoons cinnamon

Preheat the oven to 350 degrees. Sift the flour, baking powder, baking soda and salt together. Beat the margarine, 1 cup granulated sugar and the eggs in a mixing bowl until light and fluffy. Beat in the dry ingredients alternately with the sour cream and vanilla, beating well after each addition. Spread one-half of the batter into a greased and floured 9×13-inch baking pan. Combine the brown sugar, 1/2 cup granulated sugar and the cinnamon in a bowl and mix well. Sprinkle one-half over the batter in the baking pan. Top with the remaining batter and sprinkle with the remaining brown sugar mixture. Bake for 35 to 40 minutes or until a wooden pick inserted near the center comes out clean.

Stuffed Sweet Biscuits

Makes 20 biscuits

1 cup packed light brown sugar
1/4 cup (1/2 stick) butter, softened
1/3 cup light corn syrup
3/4 cup pecans, coarsely chopped
8 ounces cream cheese, softened
1/4 cup confectioners' sugar
2 tablespoons butter, softened
2 (10-count) cans buttermilk biscuits

Preheat the oven to 350 degrees. Combine the brown sugar, 1/4 cup butter, the corn syrup and pecans in a bowl and mix until crumbly. Sprinkle evenly over the bottom of a nonstick 9×13-inch baking pan. Combine the cream cheese, confectioners' sugar and 2 tablespoons butter in a bowl and mix well.

Separate each can of biscuit dough into ten biscuits on a work surface and pat each biscuit into a 4-inch circle. Spoon about 1 tablespoon of the cream cheese mixture into the center of each biscuit. Fold the sides of each biscuit over the center and pinch to seal. Arrange the biscuits seam side down in the prepared pan. Bake for 20 to 25 minutes or until light brown. Invert the baking pan onto a heatproof serving tray and remove the pan.

Jogging anyone? People in Cincinnati don't just love a good meal—many folks also like to get out and enjoy the great outdoors. The annual Flying Pig Marathon is one fantastic way to push your body to the limit while exploring the quaint neighborhoods surrounding Downtown Cincinnati. The marathon is the crown jewel of a family-friendly festival with all kinds of activities for children, including mini races and a huge pasta dinner the night before the big race.

Chocolate Zucchini Muffins

Makes 24 muffins

*A muffin that the kids will love—just don't tell them
the recipe includes vegetables.*

3 cups all-purpose flour
2 teaspoons baking soda
$1/4$ teaspoon salt
$1/2$ teaspoon cinnamon
$1/4$ teaspoon nutmeg
3 eggs
1 cup vegetable oil

2 cups sugar
2 cups grated zucchini
1 tablespoon vanilla extract
1 cup chocolate chips
1 cup walnuts, coarsely chopped
(optional)

Preheat the oven to 350 degrees. Mix the flour, baking soda, salt, cinnamon and nutmeg together. Beat the eggs, oil and sugar in a mixing bowl. Stir in the zucchini and vanilla. Add the dry ingredients and stir just until mixed. Fold in the chocolate chips and walnuts. Fill greased and floured or paper-lined muffin cups two-third full. Bake for 25 minutes or until the muffins test done.

NOTE: *It is not necessary to peel the zucchini before grating. You may also add $1/2$ cup crushed pineapple or raisins to the batter, if desired.*

Peach Applesauce Muffins

Makes 12 muffins

2 cups all-purpose flour
$3/4$ cup sugar
2 teaspoons baking powder
$3/4$ teaspoon cinnamon
$1/2$ teaspoon nutmeg

$1/4$ teaspoon salt
1 egg, lightly beaten
1 cup peach-flavor applesauce
$1/2$ cup (1 stick) butter, melted
1 firm peach, peeled and chopped

Preheat the oven to 375 degrees. Combine the flour, sugar, baking powder, cinnamon, nutmeg and salt in a bowl and mix lightly with a fork. Add the egg, applesauce and butter and stir just until combined. Fold in the peach. Fill greased or paper-lined muffin cups two-thirds full. Bake for 18 to 20 minutes or until the muffins spring back when lightly touched. Cool in the pan for 2 minutes. Remove to a wire rack to cool completely.

Cincinnati Seasoned

Pumpkin Cinnamon Chip Muffins

Makes 12 muffins

1/2 cup shortening

1 cup sugar

2 eggs

1 2/3 cups all-purpose flour

1/2 teaspoon baking soda

1/2 teaspoon baking powder

1/2 teaspoon salt

1 cup canned pumpkin

1 cup (6 ounces) cinnamon chips

Preheat the oven to 350 degrees. Beat the shortening and sugar in a mixing bowl until light and fluffy. Beat in the eggs. Add the flour, baking soda, baking powder and salt and mix well. Stir in the pumpkin. Fold in the cinnamon chips. Fill greased or paper-lined muffin cups two-third full. Bake for 20 to 23 minutes or until a wooden pick inserted in the center comes out clean.

NOTE: *One cup of white chocolate chips can be substituted for the cinnamon chips for a richer flavor.*

Zucchini Pineapple Bread

Serves 16

3 cups all-purpose flour

1 tablespoon baking soda

1 teaspoon baking powder

1 teaspoon salt

3 eggs

2 cups sugar

1 cup vegetable oil

2 teaspoons vanilla extract

2 cups grated zucchini

1 cup drained crushed pineapple

1/2 cup raisins

1 cup chopped nuts

Preheat the oven to 325 degrees. Sift the flour, baking soda, baking powder and salt together. Beat the eggs, sugar, oil and vanilla in a large mixing bowl until creamy. Add the dry ingredients and zucchini and mix well. Stir in the pineapple, raisins and nuts. Spoon into two well-greased 5×9-inch loaf pans. Bake for 1 hour or until the bread tests done. Remove to a wire rack to cool.

Bob's Mom's Banana Bread

Serves 8

2 cups all-purpose flour
1¹/2 teaspoons baking powder
1 teaspoon baking soda
¹/2 cup (1 stick) butter or margarine, softened
1 cup sugar
2 eggs
¹/4 cup sour cream
2 ripe bananas, mashed
1 cup chocolate chips

Preheat the oven to 350 degrees. Mix the flour, baking powder and baking soda together. Beat the butter and sugar in a mixing bowl until light and fluffy. Beat in the eggs. Add the sour cream and bananas and beat well. Stir in the dry ingredients. Fold in the chocolate chips. Spoon into a greased large loaf pan or two greased small loaf pans. Bake for 50 minutes or until the bread tests done. Remove to a wire rack to cool.

NOTE: *You may double the amount of chocolate chips if you really want to indulge.*

Ale Bread

Makes 1 loaf

Your whole family will love this delicious bread.

3 cups self-rising wheat flour
2 tablespoons sugar
1 (12-ounce) can light beer
2 tablespoons butter, melted

Preheat the oven to 350 degrees. Grease the bottom only of a loaf pan. Combine the flour, sugar and beer in a bowl and mix well. Pour into the prepared pan. Bake for 1 hour or until the bread tests done. Remove to a wire rack and pour the melted butter evenly over the bread in the pan. Slice the bread into bite-size pieces when cool and serve with your favorite dipping cheese.

Bob's Mom's Banana Bread was originally created by Betty Zimmerman, mother of musician Bob Dylan. Mrs. Zimmerman used to vacation in Arizona to escape Minnesota's cold winter months. That's where she passed on the recipe to her friend and fellow Duluth native, Evelyn Kuth. Mrs. Kuth has since passed on the recipe to her own family, and it is very much enjoyed by her granddaughter, Katy Crossen.

Best Country Corn Bread

Serves 9

3 eggs	1/2 cup sugar
3 cups sour cream	3/4 cup (1 1/2 sticks) butter, melted
2 1/2 cups all-purpose flour	1 cup frozen white corn kernels,
2 1/2 cups cornmeal	thawed (optional)
1 1/2 tablespoons baking powder	1/4 cup thinly sliced scallions,
1 tablespoon baking soda	green part only (optional)
2 teaspoons salt	

Preheat the oven to 350 degrees. Whisk the eggs and sour cream in a bowl. Combine the flour, cornmeal, baking powder, baking soda, salt and sugar in a large bowl and mix well. Add the egg mixture, butter, corn and scallions and stir just until mixed; the batter will be thick. Spread into a greased 9×13-inch baking dish. Bake for 30 to 40 minutes or until puffed and golden brown and a wooden pick inserted in the center comes out clean.

This recipe is from
Chef Renée Schuler
of Eat Well.

Having a quick homemade bread beats any store-bought bread hands down. The beauty of Chef Schuler's recipe is that it just gets mixed together and baked (no yeast!). Easy to mix together the afternoon of a party, and then bake it right before the guests arrive. You can serve corn bread warm from the oven and the house will smell fantastic. Add or substitute shredded Cheddar cheese and pickled jalapeño chiles for the corn kernels and scallions.

Pesto Cheese Bread

Serves 10 to 12

Cheesy, tasty, easy, and a real crowd-pleaser! This can be served in slices as an appetizer or along with a meal.

8 ounces cream cheese, softened	Pesto to taste
1 loaf French bread, sliced in	5 or 6 slices mozzarella cheese
half lengthwise	

Preheat the oven to 400 degrees. Spread equal portions of the cream cheese over the cut sides of the bread halves. Spread pesto over the cream cheese and top with the mozzarella cheese slices. Place the bread on a baking sheet. Bake for 5 to 10 minutes or until the cheese is melted and bubby. Let cool slightly. Slice and serve warm.

Grilled Flatbread with Gorgonzola and Port Caramelized Onions

Serves 8

1 tablespoon butter	2 teaspoons kosher salt
2 large red onions, cut into halves lengthwise and thinly sliced	2 flatbreads or pita rounds
	1 tablespoon olive oil
2 tablespoons port	Kosher salt to taste
2 tablespoons sugar	1 cup crumbled Gorgonzola cheese

Melt the butter in a preheated skillet over medium heat. Add the onions and cook until golden brown and beginning to stick to the bottom of the skillet, stirring occasionally. Add the wine and cook, stirring constantly and scraping up any brown bits from the bottom of the skillet. Stir in the sugar and 2 teaspoons salt and reduce the heat to low. Cook for 45 minutes or until thickened, adding up to 2 tablespoons water if the onions begin to stick to the bottom of the skillet. Adjust the seasonings to taste and let cool. Preheat the grill to medium-high. Brush the flatbreads with the olive oil and sprinkle with salt to taste. Grill the bread for 5 minutes per side. Preheat the oven to 375 degrees. Spread the onions evenly over each flatbread and top with equal portions of the cheese. Place the flatbreads on a baking sheet. Bake for 15 minutes to heat through and melt the cheese. Cut into wedges and serve.

NOTE: *The options for topping the flatbread are endless. Try marinated artichoke hearts and brie; sautéed mushrooms and fontina cheese; tomatoes, basil, and fresh mozzarella cheese or robiola; or goat cheese and truffle oil.*

This recipe is from
Chef Renée Schuler
of Eat Well.

Soups & Salads

Union Terminal

Cincinnati Union Terminal officially opened on March 31, 1933, with a crowd of 50,000 attending the dedication ceremony. The last great railroad station built in the United States, Union Terminal is considered an Art Deco masterpiece.

George Dent Crabbs, a local businessman and civic leader, negotiated with seven railroads to build a centralized terminal. He convinced the seven to jointly establish a centralized union terminal that would serve both passenger operations and freight. Architects Fellheimer and Wagner of New York City built Union Terminal in the time's popular Art Déco style, featuring a beautiful arched entrance with a large, centered clock and a fountain that greeted visitors who approached the building. It was French architect Paul Cret who provided the Art Déco elements and German artist Winold Reiss who designed several mosaic murals portraying the history of Cincinnati. Construction began in August 1929, and trains first pulled in to Union Terminal on March 19, 1933, nine months ahead of schedule.

Union Terminal operated as a passenger railroad station from 1933 until 1972; unfortunately, it was built far too late to ever see its full potential realized. By the time Cincinnati Union Terminal opened, rail travel was fading as air travel and automobiles were increasing in popularity and reliability.

After Union Terminal closed, plans were in motion to demolish the 450-foot-long concourse in 1973. A group called Save the Terminal raised more than $400,000 to cover the cost to safely remove and transport the fourteen Cincinnati worker/industry murals designed by Winold Reiss. The murals were installed at the Greater Cincinnati Northern Kentucky International Airport, where they can be seen today.

In the spring of 1973, the forward thinking of Cincinnati City Council saved the building and designated it an historic city landmark. Now Cincinnati Union Terminal houses the museum complex which includes Cincinnati History Museum, Children's Museum, Museum of Natural History and Science, and the OMNIMAX Theater.

Visit Cincinnati Museum Center at Union Terminal at www.cincymuseum.org.

Mother's Day Tea

Champagne Cocktail

Blueberry, Blue Cheese & Pecan Salad

Grape Truffles

Bob's Mom's Banana Bread

Brie with Wine Glaze

Orzo Florentine

Pear Custard Tart

Sweet Potato and Andouille Sausage Soup

Serves 6

A delicious mix of smooth and spicy flavors.

1 1/4 pounds sweet potatoes
1 tablespoon olive oil
1 cup chopped onion
1 tablespoon olive oil
1 1/2 teaspoons minced garlic
1/4 teaspoon cayenne pepper
1 Turkish bay leaf
1 teaspoon dried thyme
1 tablespoon chipotle chile powder
4 cups chicken broth
1 pound chicken andouille, cooked, drained
    and crumbled
1/2 cup heavy cream
Salt and black pepper to taste

Preheat the oven to 400 degrees. Brush the sweet potatoes with 1 tablespoon olive oil and place on a baking sheet. Bake for 1 hour or until fork-tender. Peel the potatoes when cool and discard the skins.

Sauté the onion in 1 tablespoon olive oil in a saucepan over medium-high heat until tender and translucent. Add the garlic and sauté for 30 seconds. Stir in the cayenne pepper, bay leaf, thyme, chile powder, chicken broth and 3/4 cup of the sausage. Bring to a boil; reduce the heat. Stir in the sweet potatoes. Simmer for 10 minutes. Remove from the heat. Remove and discard the bay leaf.

Purée the soup in batches in a blender or with an immersion blender. Return the soup to the saucepan and stir in the cream, salt and black pepper. Cook until heated through. Ladle into serving bowls and top with the remaining sausage.

The National Underground Railroad Freedom Center in downtown Cincinnati focuses on the history of the Underground Railroad. First Lady Laura Bush, Oprah Winfrey, and Muhammad Ali attended the groundbreaking ceremony on June 17, 2002.

Soups & Salads

Ancho Pinto Chili with Cumin Crema

Serves 8 to 10

Very different from
the more familiar Texan
chili, Cincinnati-style
chili has made the Queen
City a chili capital in
its own right. The key
to Cincinnati chili is
a thinner consistency and
an unusual blend of
flavors which sometimes
includes cinnamon
or chocolate. Locals enjoy
Cincinnati chili spooned
over freshly made pasta
and topped with a
combination of chopped
onions, shredded Cheddar
cheese, kidney beans,
and crushed oyster
crackers. The "works,"
called a Five-Way, piles on
all of those toppings.
The Four-Way is served
without the beans or
onions, and the Three-
Way is a simple dish of
noodles, chili, and cheese.

1 cup crème fraîche
1¹/2 tablespoons ground cumin
1 teaspoon kosher salt
¹/4 teaspoon pepper
1 tablespoon vegetable oil
3 pounds ground chuck
2 onions, chopped
4 garlic cloves, chopped
¹/4 cup ancho chile powder
1 tablespoon cumin
2 tomatoes, chopped
12 ounces cooked pinto beans, drained
6 cups vegetable broth
Kosher salt to taste

Whisk the crème fraîche, 1¹/2 tablespoons cumin, 1 teaspoon salt and the pepper in a bowl. Chill, covered, for 30 minutes or longer. Heat the oil in a large saucepan over high heat. Add the ground beef and cook, stirring until crumbly. Remove the ground beef with a slotted spoon to a bowl. Drain and discard all but 1 tablespoon of the drippings from the saucepan. Heat the drippings in the saucepan over high heat.

Add the onions and garlic and sauté until tender. Reduce the heat to medium-high. Add the chile powder and 1 tablespoon cumin and cook for 30 seconds, stirring constantly. Stir in the ground beef, tomatoes, beans and broth. Season with salt to taste. Bring to a boil; reduce the heat. Simmer, covered, for 45 minutes. Ladle the chili into serving bowls and top each with a dollop of the cumin crema.

White Bean Chicken Chili

Serves 6 to 8

1 small onion, chopped

3 garlic cloves, minced

1 tablespoon olive oil

3 (4-ounce) cans chopped green chiles

1 1/2 teaspoons dried oregano

2 teaspoons cumin

6 cups chicken broth

6 cups cooked Great Northern beans or
     other white beans

4 cups shredded cooked chicken

1/2 teaspoon kosher salt

1/2 teaspoon freshly ground pepper

3 cups (12 ounces) shredded Pepper Jack cheese

Sauté the onion and garlic in the olive oil in a large saucepan over medium heat until tender. Add the green chiles, oregano and cumin and mix well. Stir in the broth. Cook over medium-high heat for 15 minutes, stirring occasionally. Stir in the beans, chicken, salt and pepper. Bring to a boil; reduce the heat. Simmer, uncovered, for 10 minutes or until heated through. Add 1 1/2 cups of the cheese and cook until the cheese is melted, stirring constantly. Ladle into serving bowls and top with the remaining cheese.

NOTE: *You may use Monterey Jack cheese instead of Pepper Jack cheese for a less spicy chili.*

Cream of Brie Soup in Apple Cups

Makes 12 (¹/4- to ¹/2-cup) servings

6 large apples
¹/2 cup chopped yellow onion
¹/2 cup chopped celery
2 tablespoons butter
¹/4 cup all-purpose flour
2 cups milk
2 cups chicken broth
12 ounces Brie cheese, cut into chunks
Salt and pepper to taste
Lemon juice
12 ounces sliced toasted almonds

Cut the tops off the apples and remove the seeds and some of the pulp to form cups. Add the apple cups to a bowl of water with lemon juice added to prevent browning.

Sauté the onion and celery in the butter in a saucepan over medium heat until tender. Stir in the flour. Cook for 1 minute, stirring constantly. Whisk in the milk and broth. Cook until thickened, stirring constantly. Add the cheese and cook until the cheese is melted, stirring constantly. Remove from the heat and purée in batches in a blender. Return the soup to the saucepan and season with salt and pepper. Heat the soup over low heat until heated through.

Remove the apple cups from the water and pat dry. Ladle the soup into the apple cups and garnish with the almonds.

NOTE: *If serving this soup on a brunch table, keep the soup warm in a slow cooker and let guests serve themselves. Offer optional garnishes such as cheese or toasted bread cut with seasonal cookie cutters or seasonal spices such as pumpkin pie spice in the fall.*

Mushroom Dill Soup

Serves 2 to 4

2 tablespoons butter
2 cups chopped onions
1/4 teaspoon salt
1/4 teaspoon pepper
12 ounces fresh mushrooms, sliced
1 tablespoon minced fresh dill weed
1/2 cup chicken broth
1 tablespoon light soy sauce
1 teaspoon paprika
2 tablespoons butter
1 tablespoon all-purpose flour
1 cup milk
1 1/2 cups chicken broth
2 teaspoons fresh lemon juice
1/2 cup sour cream

Melt 2 tablespoons butter in a saucepan. Add the onions and cook until tender and light brown, stirring occasionally. Stir in the salt, pepper, mushrooms, dill weed, 1/2 cup broth, the soy sauce and paprika. Simmer, covered, for 15 minutes. Melt 2 tablespoons butter in a small saucepan over medium heat and whisk in the flour. Cook until the mixture foams and bubbles, whisking constantly. Remove from the heat and add the milk all at once. Whisk vigorously to mix. Return to the heat and cook for 10 minutes or until the white sauce is thick and smooth, whisking occasionally. Stir the white sauce into the mushroom soup. Stir in 1 1/2 cups broth. Simmer, covered, for 15 minutes. Adjust the seasonings to taste. Whisk in the lemon juice and sour cream. Cook until heated through; do not boil. Serve immediately.

Cincinnati Seasoned

Tomato and Lentil Soup

Serves 6 to 8

1 white onion, chopped

3 cups vegetable stock

1¹/2 cups cooked red or brown lentils

2 (14-ounce) cans chopped tomatoes
  with herbs

¹/4 cup mixed herbs or
  herbes de Provence

Pepper to taste

Place the onion in a microwave-safe bowl. Microwave on High for 1 minute to soften. Remove the onion to a saucepan and stir in the stock and lentils. Bring to a slow simmer. Cook, covered, for 30 minutes, stirring occasionally. Stir in the tomatoes, mixed herbs and pepper. Simmer for 30 minutes. Remove from the heat and purée in batches in a blender or with an immersion blender. Return the soup to the heat and cook for 10 minutes, adding water if the soup is too thick. Serve immediately with garlic bread or a baguette.

NOTE: *This recipe doubles easily and it freezes well.*

Tunisian Tomato Soup

Serves 6

1 teaspoon olive oil

3 garlic cloves, chopped

1 large onion, chopped

2 teaspoons cumin

1 teaspoon turmeric

1 teaspoon cinnamon

1 (15-ounce) can chick-peas, rinsed
  and drained

1 cup lentils, rinsed

1 (28-ounce) can crushed or
  diced tomatoes

2 cups water

Salt and pepper taste

Handful of cilantro, chopped

Hot red pepper flakes to taste

Heat the olive oil in a saucepan over medium heat. Add the garlic and onion and sauté for 2 minutes. Add the cumin, turmeric and cinnamon and sauté for 2 minutes. Stir in the chick-peas, lentils, tomatoes and water. Simmer for 30 minutes or until the lentils are tender. Season with salt and pepper. Serve with the cilantro and pepper flakes on the side.

This recipe is from
Cincinnati-based
www.sparkrecipes.com.

Soups & Salads

Miss Marjorie Gibson volunteering at Children's Convalescent Hospital

Bok Choy and Thai Noodle Soup

Serves 6

*Junior League of Cincinnati members traveling abroad have
discovered and fallen in love with the simple soups enjoyed by the natives
of China and Thailand. This soup is inspired by those adventures.*

2 shallots, finely chopped

1/2 garlic bulb, finely chopped

1 1/2 tablespoons extra-virgin olive oil

2 yellow onions, chopped

8 cups chicken stock

1/2 (6-ounce) package Thai
    rice noodles

3 bunches bok choy, cut into
    1/2-inch pieces

Pepper to taste

1 bunch scallions, chopped

1 bunch cilantro, chopped

Sauté the shallots and garlic in the olive oil in a large saucepan over medium-high heat until tender and beginning to brown. Add the onions and sauté for 2 to 3 minutes. Stir in the stock and reduce the heat to medium. Fill a saucepan one-half full with water and bring to a simmer over medium heat. Add the noodles and cook for 10 minutes without boiling; drain. Add the bok choy to the stock mixture and cook for 10 minutes. Add the noodles and season with pepper. Ladle into serving bowls and sprinkle with the scallions and cilantro.

Maisonette Strawberry Consommé

Serves 4 to 6

2 cups fresh strawberries

1 1/2 cups (1-inch pieces) fresh or
    frozen rhubarb

1 (3-inch) cinnamon stick

1 cup sugar

2 cups water

1/2 cup red burgundy, pinot noir
    or cabernet

1/2 cup soda water

Sour cream or plain yogurt to taste

Reserve six strawberries; set aside. Slice the remaining strawberries. Combine the sliced strawberries, rhubarb, cinnamon stick, sugar and water in a saucepan and mix well. Bring to a boil; reduce the heat. Simmer for 5 minutes or until the rhubarb is tender. Pour though a wire mesh strainer into a bowl and press the solids with a spoon to extract all of the juice to measure 3 cups. Discard the solids. Stir the wine and soda water into the juice. Ladle into bowls. Slice the reserved strawberries. Garnish the consommé with sliced strawberries and sour cream.

This consommé was served at Cincinnati's grandest restaurant, Maisonette. The downtown 6th Street classic closed its doors in 2005 after fifty-six years of business. The Maisonette was the nation's longest-running five-star restaurant, claiming that prestigious title for more than forty years.

Soups & Salads

77

Watercress, Mandarin Orange and Cashew Salad

Serves 4

2 bunches watercress, torn into
    bite-size pieces
1 (11-ounce) can mandarin
    oranges, drained
1/2 cup snow peas, strings removed
1/3 cup finely chopped green onions
1/2 cup thinly sliced jicama strips
1/2 cup cashews
3 tablespoons vegetable oil

3 tablespoons orange juice
1 teaspoon grated orange zest
1 teaspoon granulated sugar
1 teaspoon light brown sugar
1 garlic clove, finely chopped
1 teaspoon finely chopped fresh ginger
1 teaspoon soy sauce
1 teaspoon rice wine vinegar
White pepper to taste

Combine the watercress, oranges, snow peas, green onions, jicama and cashews in a large bowl and toss gently to mix. Process the oil, orange juice, orange zest, granulated sugar, brown sugar, garlic, ginger, soy sauce and vinegar in a blender until blended. Season with white pepper. Pour over the salad and toss gently to coat.

Blueberry, Blue Cheese and Pecan Salad

Serves 4

12 ounces mixed baby greens
2 tablespoons salted butter
1 cup pecan halves
1/2 cup crumbled blue cheese
1 cup fresh blueberries

Arrange equal portions of the greens on four salad plates. Melt the butter in a small skillet over medium heat. Add the pecans and sauté for 1 to 3 minutes or until light brown. Spoon equal portions of the pecans over the greens. Sprinkle each salad with 2 tablespoons of blue cheese. Arrange 1/4 cup of the blueberries on top of each salad. Serve with Raspberry Dressing (page 91).

Fresh Spinach Salad
Serves 6

*Spinach contains lutein, which is a phytochemical that
may help protect your vision.*

6 cups fresh spinach, rinsed and dried
1/3 cup thinly sliced red onion
1 Granny Smith apple, sliced
2 (11-ounce) cans mandarin oranges, drained
1/2 cup candied pecans
1 cup full-fat or nonfat vanilla yogurt
3 tablespoons red wine vinegar
1 tablespoon honey
1 tablespoon mustard

Combine the spinach and onion in a bowl and toss to mix. Add the apple, oranges and pecans and toss to mix. Chill for up to 1 hour. Whisk the yogurt, vinegar, honey and mustard in a bowl. Add to the salad and toss to coat or serve the yogurt dressing on the side.

Cabbage Carrot Slaw
Serves 12

4 cups shredded cabbage
4 cups shredded carrots
1 cup raisins
1 cup mayonnaise
1/4 cup honey
1 teaspoon grated lemon zest
1/4 cup fresh lemon juice
1/2 teaspoon ground ginger

Combine the cabbage, carrots and raisins in a large bowl. Whisk the mayonnaise, honey, lemon zest, lemon juice and ginger in a bowl. Add to the cabbage mixture and toss to coat. Chill until cold.

Cincinnati Seasoned

Savory Red Potato Salad

Serves 6

1 lemon
3 or 4 ribs celery, finely chopped
1/2 red onion, finely chopped
2 to 3 tablespoons drained capers
1/4 to 1/2 cup olive oil
1 pound red potatoes
Salt to taste
1/2 cup mayonnaise
Pepper to taste
2 tablespoons chopped fresh parsley or basil

Grate the zest from the lemon and set aside. Juice the lemon into a small bowl. Combine the lemon juice, celery, onion, capers and olive oil in a large bowl and mix well. Cook the potatoes in a saucepan of boiling salted water until tender; drain.

Peel the potatoes immediately and cut into bite-size pieces. Add the warm potatoes to the olive oil mixture and toss to coat. Add the mayonnaise, salt and pepper and toss to mix. Garnish with the parsley and lemon zest.

NOTE: *It is important to toss the potatoes with the dressing while the potatoes are still warm so they can soak up the dressing!*

The Junior League of Cincinnati was founded in 1920 and is part of a network of more than 294 Junior League Organizations in the United States, Canada, Mexico, and Great Britain. The Association of Junior Leagues International, Inc., founded in 1901, has more than 170,000 members. Our organization is committed to improving our community by stimulating change and empowering people through the direct efforts of our dedicated volunteers. Our members are global in complexion and perspective. Our League strives to partner with the community and strengthen our ability to make an impact on the lives of those we serve.

Savory Watermelon Salad

Serves 8

2 tablespoons rice wine vinegar

2 tablespoons olive oil

3 to 4 cups watermelon chunks

4 ounces crumbled feta cheese

4 dashes of pepper (or to taste)

Whisk the vinegar and olive oil in a bowl. Add the watermelon, cheese and pepper and toss to mix. Serve slightly chilled but avoid making too far ahead or the salad will become soggy.

NOTE: *Try using blue cheese, mixed melons, and/or adding fresh savory herbs.*

Fresh Couscous Salad

Serves 4

1 (5-ounce) package couscous

1 bunch asparagus, chopped

2 green onions, chopped

1 cup grape tomatoes or
    cherry tomatoes

8 ounces cooked peeled small shrimp

1/4 cup (or more) chicken broth

3 tablespoons lemon juice

1 tablespoon olive oil

Salt and pepper to taste

Cook the couscous according to the package directions, adding the asparagus during the last 5 minutes of cooking. Remove to a bowl. Stir in the green onions, tomatoes and shrimp. Whisk 1/4 cup broth, the lemon juice, olive oil, salt and pepper in a bowl. Add to the couscous and mix well. Chill until cold. Add additional broth is the mixture seems too dry.

NOTE: *In lieu of packaged couscous, place 3/4 cup bulk couscous in a bowl and pour 1 1/4 cups boiling water over the couscous. Add the asparagus and let stand for 5 minutes. You may also add crushed garlic for a different flavor.*

Herbed Orzo Salad
Serves 8

DRESSING

2 teaspoons grated lemon zest
1/4 cup fresh lemon juice
1 teaspoon minced garlic
3/4 cup olive oil
Salt and pepper to taste

SALAD

Salt to taste
6 ounces sugar snap peas, cut into 3/4-inch pieces
2 2/3 cups orzo
1 1/4 cups chopped seeded tomatoes
3/4 cup chopped seeded peeled cucumber
1/2 cup chopped green onions
1/4 cup chopped fresh mint
2 teaspoons grated lemon zest
1/4 cup chopped fresh parsley
Pepper to taste

For the dressing, mix the lemon zest, lemon juice and garlic in a bowl. Whisk in the olive oil gradually. Season with salt and pepper.

For the salad, bring a large saucepan of salted water to a boil. Add the snow peas and boil for 1 minute. Remove the snow peas with a wire strainer to a colander and rinse with cold water. Add the orzo to the saucepan of boiling water. Cook for 8 minutes or until al dente; drain and let cool. Combine the snow peas, orzo, tomatoes, cucumber, green onions, mint, lemon zest, parsley, salt and pepper in a bowl and toss to mix. Add one-half of the dressing and toss to coat. Chill, covered, for up to 6 hours. Chill the remaining dressing. Bring the salad to room temperature when ready to serve. Add enough of the remaining dressing to coat and toss to mix.

Pizza Pasta Salad

Serves 6

16 ounces multigrain penne (or favorite pasta)

1 tablespoon olive oil

1/2 (6-ounce) package reduced-fat pepperoni,
    cut into quarters

1 (7-ounce) jar sliced black olives, drained

1/2 cup chopped Vidalia onion

1/2 (12-ounce) jar roasted red peppers, drained
    and chopped

1 (7-ounce) jar sliced mushrooms, drained

1 cup cherry tomatoes or grape tomatoes,
    cut into quarters

1/4 cup chopped green bell pepper

1 teaspoon oregano

1/2 teaspoon basil

Salt to taste

Grated Parmesan cheese (optional)

Cook the pasta using the package directions; drain and let cool. Combine the pasta and olive oil in a large bowl and toss to coat. Add the pepperoni, olives, onion, roasted red peppers, mushrooms, tomatoes, bell pepper, oregano and basil and toss to mix. Chill for at least 2 hours. Season with salt and sprinkle with cheese.

Junior League of Cincinnati's Columbia Center has deep roots in the community. The structure first opened its doors after a grand ceremony in September 1904. The impressive three-story, red brick building with a large window, elegant lighting, fixtures, and a main door facing Columbia Parkway was the center of attention in the neighborhood. Originally home of the Yeatman Masonic Temple, the most impressive features of the time were the large figures made of stained glass looking out onto Columbia Tusculm.

Soups & Salads

Shrimp and Cucumber Salad
Serves 4

1 cup water
1 cup white wine
Juice and zest of 1 lemon
1 pound peeled fresh shrimp
1/2 cup mayonnaise
1/2 cup chopped red onion
2 tablespoons lemon juice
1 tablespoon chopped fresh parsley
1 tablespoon chopped fresh dill weed
2 teaspoons Splenda
1 cup chopped seeded peeled cucumber

Bring the water, wine, juice of one lemon and the lemon zest to a simmer in a saucepan. Add the shrimp and cook for 3 minutes or until the shrimp turn pink. Drain and let cool. Cut the shrimp into bite-size pieces. Combine the mayonnaise, onion, 2 tablespoons lemon juice, the parsley, dill weed, artificial sweetener and cucumber in a bowl and mix well. Add the shrimp and mix well. Chill, covered, overnight.

Sweet–and–Savory Chicken Salad
Serves 6

4 to 6 boneless skinless chicken breasts
1 (14-ounce) can chicken broth
1/2 cup chopped celery
2 tablespoons chopped onion
1 cup dried cranberries
2 cups mayonnaise
1/4 cup honey
2 tablespoons poppy seeds
1 tablespoon balsamic vinegar

Simmer the chicken in the broth in a saucepan over low heat for 2 hours; drain. Shred the chicken immediately. Combine the hot chicken, celery, onion, cranberries, mayonnaise, honey, poppy seeds and vinegar in a bowl and mix well. Let cool to room temperature. Chill until cold.

Mediterranean Orzo Salad

Serves 4

Serve this as an entrée salad topped with chopped grilled chicken or grilled shrimp. It also makes a wonderful side dish to any grilled protein.

1/4 cup pine nuts

1/4 cup olive oil

2 tablespoons fresh lemon juice

1 1/2 teaspoons minced garlic

1/2 teaspoon dried oregano

1/2 teaspoon salt

1/8 teaspoon freshly ground pepper

1/2 teaspoon sugar

Salt to taste

1 cup regular or wheat orzo

3 tablespoons finely chopped black olives

1 1/2 to 2 tablespoons finely chopped red onion
   (or to taste)

1/4 cup thin basil strips

2 ounces feta cheese, coarsely crumbled

2 chicken breasts, grilled and chopped (optional)

4 or 5 sprigs basil for garnish

Toast the pine nuts in a small skillet over medium-low heat, stirring constantly; let cool. Whisk the olive oil, lemon juice, garlic, oregano, 1/2 teaspoon salt, the pepper and sugar in a bowl. Bring a large saucepan of salted water to a boil. Add the orzo and cook for 8 to 10 minutes or until al dente. Drain and rinse with cold water for just a few seconds. Remove the hot orzo to a large bowl. Add the olive oil mixture immediately and toss to coat. Let cool to room temperature, stirring occasionally. Stir in the pine nuts, olives, onion and 1/4 cup basil. Add the cheese and toss to mix. Adjust the seasonings to taste. Top with the chicken. Garnish with the basil sprigs and serve.

NOTE: *This is a great dish to make for parties, either the night before or morning of the event. If you make it in advance, reserve one-half of the basil strips and basil garnish and add just before serving.*

Autumn Chicken Salad

Serves 6

3 pounds boneless skinless
  chicken breasts

3/4 cup chopped celery

3/4 cup pecan pieces

1 1/4 cups seedless green grape halves

3/4 cup dried cranberries

1/4 cup chopped onion

3 cups mayonnaise

Kosher salt to taste

Poppy seeds to taste

Preheat the oven to 350 degrees. Arrange the chicken in baking pan and add water to measure 1 inch. Bake, covered with foil, for 30 to 40 minutes or until the chicken is cooked through. Remove the chicken to a work surface and cut into bite-size pieces. Combine the chicken, celery, pecans, grapes, cranberries and onion in a bowl and toss to mix. Add the mayonnaise, salt and poppy seeds and mix well. Replace some of the mayonnaise with the cooking broth if you wish to reduce the amount of mayonnaise. Serve as a sandwich filling or on lettuce leaves. Spoon the salad into endive leaves for an appetizer or brunch dish.

NOTE: *For more flavorful chicken, use 3 1/2 pounds whole chicken breasts with the skin on. Sprinkle kosher salt under the skin and add only a small amount of water to the baking pan. Remove and discard the skin and bones after the chicken is cooked.*

Asian Balsamic Dressing

Makes 3/4 cup

A new twist on an old favorite! This recipe gives your favorite balsamic stand-by the flavor of the Far East.

3 or 4 garlic cloves

1/2 teaspoon coarse salt

1/4 cup balsamic vinegar

2/3 cup extra-virgin olive oil

2 tablespoons fresh lemon juice

2 teaspoons soy sauce

1 teaspoon sugar

1 1/2 teaspoons grated fresh ginger

Pepper to taste

Mash the garlic and salt in a bowl to make a paste. Whisk in the vinegar, olive oil, lemon juice, soy sauce, sugar, ginger and pepper. Serve over your favorite salad. Store any remaining dressing in a covered container in the refrigerator.

Cincinnati Seasoned

Blue Cheese Dressing

Makes 3 cups

Skip a trip down the dressing aisle at the grocery store.
Follow these simple steps to serve up a fresh, flavorful dressing
that's sure to become a family favorite.

8 ounces cream cheese, softened
1 cup mayonnaise
1 cup buttermilk
1 teaspoon garlic salt
1 teaspoon onion salt
1 teaspoon pepper
3 ounces blue cheese, crumbled
Salt to taste

Beat the cream cheese, mayonnaise, buttermilk, garlic salt, onion salt and pepper in a bowl until smooth. Stir in the blue cheese and season with salt. Serve with buffalo wings.

Champagne Salad Dressing

Makes about 4 cups

2 cups olive oil
1 teaspoon dry mustard
1 teaspoon celery seeds
2 teaspoons salt
1/2 cup cider vinegar
3/4 cup sugar
1 large onion, cut into chunks
1/2 cup dry Champagne

Combine the olive oil, dry mustard, celery seeds, salt, vinegar, sugar, onion and Champagne in a blender and process until smooth and creamy. Chill, covered, for 1 hour or longer. Serve with a salad of crisp lettuces, chopped red onion, dried cranberries, walnut pieces and crumbled feta cheese.

Cincinnati Seasoned

Fresh Italian Vinaigrette

Makes 1 cup

1 garlic clove, minced
1 teaspoon minced white onion
1 teaspoon sugar
1 teaspoon salt
1/4 teaspoon freshly ground pepper
2 teaspoons minced fresh thyme
1 tablespoon minced fresh basil
3 tablespoons minced fresh oregano
1 tablespoon minced fresh parsley
1 teaspoon water
2 tablespoons white vinegar
1/2 cup extra-light olive oil

Combine the garlic, onion, sugar, salt, pepper, thyme, basil, oregano, parsley, water, vinegar and olive oil in a jar with a tight-fitting lid and shake well. Store in the refrigerator and shake well before each use.

NOTE: *To make Creamy Italian Dressing, combine all the ingredients except the olive oil in a blender. Add 1 egg and 2 tablespoons grated romano cheese and pulse until blended. Add the oil, processing constantly. If you are concerned about using raw eggs, use eggs pasteurized in their shells, which are sold at some specialty food stores, or use an equivalent amount of pasteurized egg substitute.*

Raspberry Dressing

Serves 6 to 8

1/4 cup raspberry vinegar
1/3 cup fresh or thawed frozen raspberries
1/3 cup honey
1/2 cup olive oil

Process the vinegar, raspberries and honey in a blender at high speed for 1 minute. Reduce the speed to medium and add the olive oil slowly, processing constantly until thickened.

Soups & Salads

Entrées

Krohn Conservatory

When Cincinnatians are looking for a tropical, vibrant escape, they need look no further than Krohn Conservatory in Eden Park. The classic glass structure is one of the most prominent and recognizable landmarks of Cincinnati's City Park System. The magnificent building is free and open to the public 365 days a year.

The Conservatory showcases more than 3,500 plant species from all over the world, displayed in both permanent and visiting exhibits.

Each exhibit is outstanding and unique in and of itself. The Palm House, for example, mimics a tropical rain forest and includes a twenty-foot waterfall into a stream surrounded by forty-five–foot tall trees as well as many

lower shrubs and trees. The indoor Desert Garden houses thousands of species of succulents. The Orchid Display shows a great variety of blooming orchids at their peaks. There is even an outstanding display of artistically-created bonsai in the Bonsai Collection.

The Conservatory, completed in 1933, was named in honor of Irwin M. Krohn, who served on the Board of Commissioners from 1912 to 1948. It is available to rent for weddings or special events and makes a wonderful backdrop for a memorable evening or visit to this spectacular Cincinnati resource.

You can discover Krohn Conservatory yourself by visiting www.cincinnati-oh.gov/ cityparks/ pages/-3452-/.

Holiday Celebration

Champagne Wine Punch

Prosciutto & Gruyère Pinwheels

Cream of Brie Soup in Apple Cups

Watercress, Mandarin Orange & Cashew Salad

Pork Medallions & Red Pepper Sauce

Peppermint Chocolate Icebox Cake

Beef Burgundy

Serves 8 to 10

5 pounds beef chuck roast, trimmed
    and cut into cubes
2 tablespoons canola oil
Kosher salt and freshly
    ground pepper to taste
3 tablespoons butter
1/2 cup pinot noir
1/4 cup (1/2 stick) butter
3 shallots, minced
5 garlic cloves, minced
1 tablespoon tomato paste
1/3 cup all-purpose flour

3 cups pinot noir
2 cups homemade beef stock or
    canned chicken broth
2 each thyme sprigs and parsley sprigs
1 bay leaf
1 tablespoon butter
2 cups small button mushrooms or
    halved larger mushrooms
2 tablespoons butter
1/2 bag frozen pearl onions, thawed
Beurre Manié (optional) (see sidebar)
2 tablespoons brandy

Two nights before serving, combine the beef, canola oil, salt and pepper in a bowl and toss to coat. Chill, covered, overnight. Brown the beef in three batches in a Dutch oven using 1 tablespoon butter for each batch. Remove the beef to a large bowl. Add 1/2 cup wine to the pan and cook over high heat until the liquid is reduced by one-half, stirring constantly and scraping up any brown bits from the bottom of the pan. Add to the beef. Preheat the oven to 350 degrees.

Melt 1/4 cup butter in the Dutch oven over medium heat. Add the shallots and garlic and sauté for several minutes or until beginning to brown. Add the tomato paste and cook for 1 minute, stirring constantly. Whisk in the flour and cook for 30 seconds, whisking constantly. Whisk in 3 cups wine and the stock gradually. Cook until the mixture begins to thicken, whisking constantly. Stir in the thyme, parsley and bay leaf and bring to a simmer. Stir in the beef mixture. Bake, covered loosely with foil, for 2 1/2 to 3 1/2 hours or until the beef is very tender. Let cool, uncovered, for 30 minutes. Chill, covered, overnight.

Simmer the stew over low heat. Melt 1 tablespoon butter in a skillet. Add the mushrooms and sauté until golden brown. Season with salt and pepper and remove to a bowl. Melt 2 tablespoons butter in the skillet. Add the onions and sauté until golden brown. Add to the mushrooms. Drain the liquid from the stew into a saucepan, reserving the beef. Cook until the sauce is reduced or thicken with Beurre Manié. Add to the beef; stir in the mushrooms and onions. Stir in the brandy. Cook until heated through. Remove and discard the thyme, parsley and bay leaf.

This recipe is from
Chef Renée Schuler
of Eat Well.

To make Beurre Manié, combine 2 tablespoons butter, softened with 3 tablespoons all-purpose flour in a bowl and mix well. Add one-third of the mixture to the simmering stew liquid. Cook until thickened, adding more as needed.

Braciole

Serves 4

Other great meats to use would be capicola, mortadella, Milano salami, or classic salami. If you don't have kitchen twine, you can use unflavored dental floss. Make sure it is UNflavored!

1 (1¹/2- to 2-pound) flank steak
4 ounces sliced pepperoni
4 ounces sliced prosciutto
4 ounces Genoa salami
4 ounces sliced provolone cheese or mozzarella cheese
2 tablespoons olive oil
2 (24-ounce) jars marinara sauce

Place the flank steak on a work surface with the muscle running vertically. Layer the pepperoni, prosciutto, salami and cheese in overlapping slices to cover the steak. Roll up the steak tightly from the left side, keeping the meat and cheese within the steak, and place seam side down on the work surface. Cut four lengths of kitchen twine and tie tightly at evenly spaced intervals to secure. Tie a piece of kitchen twine lengthwise around the braciole.

Heat a large saucepan over high heat and pour in the olive oil. Add the braciole when the olive oil is hot. Brown all sides. Reduce the heat to low and add the marinara sauce. Simmer, covered, for 40 to 60 minutes, stirring occasionally. Remove the braciole to a cutting board and let rest for 5 minutes. Remove the twine and slice the braciole. Serve with your favorite cooked pasta tossed in the marinara sauce.

This recipe is from
Chef Caitlyn MacEachen Steininger
of "Cooking with Caitlyn."

Beef Tenderloin Sandwich with Grilled Portobello Mushrooms

Serves 4

This is a very tender dish with a variety of flavors incorporated into the sandwich.
It's an attractive and sophisticated sandwich that anyone will enjoy.

1 (1¹/2-pound) beef tenderloin	2 ounces crumbled blue cheese
Extra-virgin olive oil	¹/3 cup mayonnaise
Sea salt and freshly ground pepper	¹/3 cup chopped pecans
to taste	¹/4 cup fresh parsley
4 portobello mushroom caps	1 loaf ciabatta bread, sliced in
¹/4 cup sun-dried tomatoes	half horizontally
4 ounces cream cheese, softened	

Preheat the broiler. Rub the tenderloin with olive oil, salt and pepper and place on a broiler pan. Broil for 4 minutes per side for medium-rare. Remove to a cutting board and let stand. Cut the tenderloin into ¹/2-inch slices. Arrange the mushrooms on the broiler pan. Drizzle with olive oil and sprinkle with salt and pepper. Broil the mushrooms for 5 minutes per side. Combine the tomatoes, cream cheese, blue cheese, mayonnaise, pecans and parsley in a food processor and process until blended. Toast the bread and spread the tomato mixture equally over the cut sides of the bread halves. Layer the sliced tenderloin and mushrooms over one-half of the bread. Top with the remaining bread half and cut into four sandwiches.

NOTE: *This recipe contains nuts for anyone who may be allergic.*

The idea of the "Junior League Cookbook" became popular in the 1950s. In that era, leagues used their time and talents to promote remedial reading centers, programs for the gifted and challenged, and the development of educational television.

Entrées

"The Wizard of Oz," presented by the Players of the Junior League of Cincinnati—1925–1926

Enchilada Casserole

Serves 6

2 tablespoons vegetable oil
1 onion, finely chopped
2 garlic cloves, minced
1 pound ground beef
1¹/2 cups salsa
1 teaspoon oregano
1 teaspoon chili powder
1 teaspoon cumin
1 tablespoon butter
1 tablespoon vegetable oil
2 cups corn kernels
1/4 cup chopped green bell pepper
1/4 cup chopped red bell pepper
6 (7-inch) corn or flour tortillas
2 cups sour cream
1 cup (4 ounces) shredded Monterey Jack cheese
1 cup (4 ounces) shredded Cheddar cheese

Heat 2 tablespoons oil in a saucepan over low heat. Add the onion and garlic and sauté until tender. Add the ground beef and cook, stirring until crumbly; drain. Stir in the salsa, oregano, chili powder and cumin. Bring to a boil; reduce the heat. Simmer for 5 minutes, stirring occasionally. Remove from the heat.

Heat the butter and 1 tablespoon oil in a skillet over low heat. Add the corn and sauté for 3 minutes. Add the bell peppers and sauté for 2 minutes or until tender. Preheat the oven to 375 degrees. Layer the tortillas, ground beef mixture, sour cream, Monterey Jack cheese and Cheddar cheese one-third at a time in an oval 2-quart baking dish. Spoon the corn mixture around the edge. Bake for 20 minutes.

Established in 1963, the Choral Group is the Junior League of Cincinnati's oldest ongoing project. Through song and dance, Choral Group provides entertainment to senior citizens in local assisted living, senior centers, and nursing homes. This project is unique in that it is comprised of community volunteers as well as Active and Sustainer JLC members.

Entrées

Meat Loaf with Sun-Dried Tomatoes and Red Currant Wine Sauce

Serves 8 to 10

2 1/2 pounds ground beef

1/2 cup Italian-style bread crumbs

1 cup finely chopped onion

1 cup grated fresh Parmesan cheese

1/2 cup thinly sliced fresh basil

1/2 cup chopped sun-dried tomatoes

1/4 cup chopped fresh parsley

4 garlic cloves, minced

2 eggs

1/2 cup red or black currant jelly

1/4 cup dry red wine

1 tablespoon all-purpose flour

Preheat the oven to 400 degrees. Combine the ground beef, bread crumbs, onion, cheese, basil, sun-dried tomatoes, parsley, garlic and eggs in a bowl and mix well. Spoon into two loaf pans coated with nonstick cooking spray. Bake for 50 minutes or until cooked through. Mix the jelly, wine and flour in a saucepan. Cook until slightly thickened, stirring constantly. Pour equal portions of the wine sauce over each meat loaf and serve.

Steak Marinade

Makes 3/4 cup

1 tablespoon fresh lemon juice

1/2 cup soy sauce

1/2 teaspoon Worcestershire sauce

1 teaspoon sugar

1/2 garlic clove, minced

2 tablespoons high-quality bourbon

Dash of Tabasco sauce

Whisk the lemon juice, soy sauce, Worcestershire sauce, sugar, garlic, bourbon and Tabasco sauce in a shallow dish. Add steaks and turn to coat. Marinate in the refrigerator for at least 45 minutes, turning occasionally. Remove the steaks and reserve the marinade. Grill or broil the steaks to desired doneness, brushing with the reserved marinade while cooking. Discard any remaining marinade.

NOTE: *This marinade is best with charcoal-grilled steaks or London broil.*

Cincinnati Seasoned

Brie and Chutney–Stuffed Pork Tenderloin with Coconut Curry Cream Sauce

Serves 6

Let your taste buds take a trip around the world as you serve up the savory spices of the Far East in a dish that puts a new spin on an old tradition.

1 (2-pound) pork tenderloin
1 cup mango chutney
1/2 (6-inch) round Brie cheese, thinly sliced
1/2 cup finely chopped pistachios
1 cup heavy cream
1 cup coconut milk
1 teaspoon curry powder
1/4 cup flaked coconut
Salt to taste

Preheat the oven to 450 degrees. Cut the tenderloin horizontally three-fourths of the way through the meat and lay open on plastic wrap. Cover with plastic wrap and pound with a meat mallet to 1/2 inch thick. Remove the plastic wrap. Spread the chutney over the tenderloin and arrange the cheese slices over the chutney. Sprinkle with the pistachios. Roll up the tenderloin tightly from the long side, keeping the filling enclosed, and tie with kitchen twine at evenly spaced intervals to secure. Place the tenderloin in a shallow roasting pan.

Bake for 25 minutes or until a meat thermometer inserted into the thickest portion of the tenderloin registers 165 degrees. Remove to a serving platter and cover with foil. Heat the cream and coconut milk in a saucepan over medium-high heat until the mixture begins to boil. Reduce the heat to medium and stir in the curry powder. Stir in the coconut and salt. Simmer until the sauce is thickened. Slice the tenderloin and serve with the curry cream sauce.

The Cincinnati Tennis Club was founded in 1880, just five years after tennis was introduced in America, and is one of the oldest active tennis clubs in the United States.

Tangerine Pork with Thyme

Serves 4

4 tangerines
4 boneless pork chops
2 pinches of salt
2 pinches of pepper
1 1/2 teaspoons vegetable oil
1 1/2 teaspoons chopped fresh thyme, or
    1/2 teaspoon dried thyme
2 tablespoons orange liqueur
2/3 cup vegetable broth
1 tablespoon cornstarch
1 green onion, sliced
Additional fresh thyme for garnish

Grate 1/2 teaspoon of zest from the tangerines and set aside. Juice two tangerines to make 1/3 cup of juice and set aside. Peel, section and remove the seeds of the remaining two tangerines and set aside. Sprinkle both sides of the pork chops with equal portions of the salt and pepper. Coat a large nonstick skillet with cooking spray. Add the oil and heat over medium heat until hot. Add the pork chops and cook for 5 minutes per side or just until cooked through and golden brown. Remove the pork chops with tongs to a plate.

Add 1 1/2 teaspoons thyme and the tangerine zest to the skillet and cook for 2 to 3 minutes, stirring constantly. Stir in the tangerine juice and orange liqueur. Stir the broth into the cornstarch in a small bowl and add to the skillet. Bring to a boil over medium heat, stirring constantly. Cook until the mixture begins to thicken, stirring constantly. Add the pork chops, tangerine sections and green onion and cook until heated through, stirring occasionally. Serve garnished with additional fresh thyme.

The nickname Porkopolis was given to Cincinnati around 1835, when the city was the country's chief hog packing center and herds of pigs roamed the streets freely.

Stuffed Pork Chops with Sage Crisps

Serves 4

This is a moist, savory bread pudding dressing.

$^1/_2$ cup (1 stick) butter

12 fresh sage leaves

$^1/_2$ cup frozen chopped onion

1$^1/_2$ cups chopped celery

2 tablespoons dried sage

1 cup chicken broth

8 to 10 slices white or whole wheat
     bread, cubed (about 4 cups)

1 egg, beaten

$^1/_2$ to 1 cup milk

4 thick boneless pork loin chops

Preheat the oven to 400 degrees. Melt the butter in a cast-iron skillet over medium heat and remove from the heat. Dip the sage leaves in the melted butter to coat and arrange in a shallow baking pan. Bake for 10 to 12 minutes or until crisp. Remove to a wire rack to cool.

Add the onion, celery and dried sage to the remaining butter in the skillet and sauté over medium heat for 8 to 10 minutes or until the vegetables are tender. Stir in the broth and cook until heated through. Pour over the bread cubes in a bowl and mix well. Stir in the egg gradually. Add the milk gradually and mix with your hands, adding enough milk to make a moist but not soggy stuffing.

Cut a 3-inch horizontal slit into the thickest portion of each pork chop to create a pocket. Fill the pockets tightly with the bread stuffing and secure the openings with wooden picks. Spoon the leftover stuffing into a baking dish. Preheat the oven to 350 degrees. Brown the pork chops on both sides in a cast-iron skillet over high heat. Remove the pork chops to a 9×13-inch baking pan. Spoon the remaining stuffing beside the pork chops or into a separate baking pan. Bake the pork chops and additional stuffing for 45 minutes or until a meat thermometer inserted into the thickest portion of the pork chop registers 160 degrees. Serve the pork chops garnished with the sage crisps.

NOTE: *One piece of bread equals approximately $^1/_2$ cup when torn and cubed. If wheat bread is used, it will absorb more liquid, so more milk or broth may be needed. Fresh sage is not as pungent as dried sage. The baked sage crisps as garnish are a treat when serving for company.*

Pork Medallions with Red Pepper Sauce

Serves 2 or 3

4 or 5 thin boneless center-cut pork chops
1/4 teaspoon Italian seasoning
1/8 teaspoon salt
1/8 teaspoon coarsely ground pepper
1 tablespoon vegetable oil
2 cups red bell pepper strips
1 cup chicken broth
3 tablespoons tomato paste
1/2 teaspoon dried thyme
1/2 teaspoon rubbed sage

Sprinkle the pork chops with the Italian seasoning, salt and pepper. Heat the oil in a large nonstick skillet over medium-high heat. Add the pork chops and cook for 2 to 3 minutes per side or until light brown. Remove the pork chops with tongs to a plate. Add the bell peppers to the skillet and sauté for 3 to 4 minutes or until tender-crisp. Return the pork chops to the skillet.

Whisk the broth, tomato paste, thyme and sage in a bowl and add to the skillet. Reduce the heat and cover the skillet. Simmer for 8 to 10 minutes or until the pork is cooked through. Remove the pork chops with tongs to a serving plate and keep warm. Increase the heat to medium-high. Cook the sauce for 3 to 4 minutes or until thickened. Spoon the sauce over the pork chops and serve.

NOTE: *You may serve the pork chops over your favorite pasta, if desired.*

British Jambalaya
Serves 4

1 large onion, chopped
3 ribs celery, chopped
1 green bell pepper, chopped
2 garlic cloves, crushed
2 tablespoons vegetable oil
8 ounces smoked sausage, chopped

1 1/3 cups rice
2 2/3 cups chicken stock, heatedd
1/2 teaspoon cayenne pepper
2 beefsteak tomatoes, chopped
8 ounces peeled cooked prawns or
　　small shrimp

Sauté the onion, celery, bell pepper and garlic in the oil in a saucepan for 5 minutes or until the vegetables are tender. Add the sausage and sauté for 3 minutes. Stir in the rice, stock, cayenne pepper and tomatoes.

Cook, covered, over high heat for 20 minutes or until the rice is tender but has a slight bite. Stir in the prawns and cook for 3 minutes. Remove from the heat and let stand for 5 minutes before serving.

New Year's Eve Ham Sandwiches
Serves 16

1/4 cup (1/2 stick)
　　margarine, softened
1 teaspoon dried onion flakes
1/4 teaspoon poppy seeds
1 teaspoon spicy mustard

2 tablespoons mayonnaise
2 (8-count) packages small bakery
　　egg rolls, split
8 slices Swiss cheese, cut into halves
16 slices deli ham

Preheat the oven to 350 degrees. Combine the margarine, onion flakes, poppy seeds, mustard and mayonnaise in a bowl and mix well. Spread equal portions of the mayonnaise mixture over the cut sides of the rolls. Top the bottom half of each roll with one slice of cheese and one slice of ham and replace the top of the rolls.

Arrange the sandwiches in a baking dish and cover the dish with foil. Bake for 20 minutes and serve warm.

Lamb Kabobs

Serves 6 to 8

8 long sprigs of rosemary
2 garlic cloves
1 tablespoon paprika
1/2 teaspoon cumin seeds
2 teaspoons coriander seeds
Dash of salt
Dash of pepper
1 tablespoon grated lemon zest
5 tablespoons extra-virgin olive oil
1 pound lamb cubes
2 red onions, cut into bite-size pieces
2 yellow bell peppers, cut into bite-size pieces

Remove the leaves from the rosemary and set the stems aside. Crush the rosemary leaves, garlic, paprika, cumin, coriander, salt and pepper in a mortar with a pestle and remove to a small bowl. Stir in the lemon zest and olive oil to make a paste. Spread the paste over the lamb in a bowl and stir to coat. Chill, covered, for 1 hour or longer. Preheat the grill to medium. Thread the lamb, onion and bell pepper alternately onto the reserved rosemary stems or metal skewers and place on the grill rack. Grill for 5 minutes or until charred on the outside and the lamb is pink on the inside, turning frequently. Remove to a serving plate and let rest for a few minutes.

NOTE: *Feel free to substitute any fresh veggies you may prefer to onion and bell pepper.*

Asparagus Chicken Roll-Ups

Serves 4

This recipe makes a wonderful, elegant statement at any dinner party.
It's easily prepared but has a "gourmet" touch.

4 boneless skinless chicken breasts
1/4 cup mild poultry seasoning
4 asparagus spears, cut into halves

1 cup (or more) crumbled feta cheese
Salt and pepper to taste

Preheat the oven to 400 degrees. Pound the chicken between sheets of waxed paper with a meat mallet until flattened. Coat both sides of the chicken with the poultry seasoning and lay the chicken on a work surface. Arrange two asparagus spear halves in the center of each chicken breast and sprinkle with equal portions of the cheese. Roll up the chicken and secure each roll-up with four wooden picks. Arrange the chicken in a baking dish coated with nonstick cooking spray. Sprinkle lightly with salt and pepper. Bake for 20 minutes or until the chicken is golden brown and cooked through.

NOTE: *You may use green, red, or yellow bell peppers instead of asparagus.*

Bistro Chicken Strips

Serves 4

1 pound chicken tenders
Sea salt and pepper to taste
1/2 cup all-purpose flour

1/2 cup Dijon mustard
1 cup herb-seasoned stuffing mix
Vegetable oil

Season both sides of the chicken with salt and pepper. Place the flour in a shallow bowl, the Dijon mustard in a small bowl and the stuffing mix in a shallow bowl. Dredge each chicken tender in the flour and shake off any excess. Dip into the Dijon mustard and coat in the stuffing mix. Heat 1 inch of oil in a 12-inch skillet over medium-high heat. Add four of the chicken tenders and fry for 3 to 4 minutes per side or until golden brown and cooked through. Remove with tongs to paper towels to drain. Repeat with the remaining chicken tenders.

Chicken Cordon Bleu

Serve 4

4 boneless skinless chicken breasts
1 envelope savory herb with garlic
    soup mix
2 tablespoons water

1/3 cup mayonnaise or olive oil
4 slices thick-cut ham
4 slices thick-cut Lorraine
    Swiss cheese

Preheat the oven to 350 degrees. Pound the chicken breasts on a work surface with a meat mallet or rolling pin to 1 inch thick. Mix the soup mix, water and mayonnaise in a bowl. Spread some of the mayonnaise mixture over each chicken breast. Arrange one slice of ham and one slice of cheese over each chicken breast. Roll up the chicken and secure each with wooden picks. Arrange the chicken rolls in a square baking dish. Bake for 20 to 30 minutes or until the chicken is cooked through, brushing with the remaining mayonnaise mixture halfway through baking.

Chicken with Champagne Glaze

Serves 2 to 4

3 tablespoons butter
2 whole boneless skinless
    chicken breasts, flattened
Salt and pepper to taste
1 cup chicken stock
1 cup brut or extra-brut Champagne,
    at room temperature
1/4 cup dry white wine

2 tablespoons minced shallots
2 tablespoons madeira
2 tablespoons minced fresh parsley
1 tablespoon minced fresh tarragon
2 tablespoons butter
2 tablespoons drained water-pack
    capers for garnish

Melt 3 tablespoons butter in a skillet over medium heat. Add the chicken and sprinkle with salt and pepper. Cook for 2 to 3 minutes per side or until cooked through. Remove the chicken with tongs to a plate. Stir the stock, Champagne, white wine and shallots into the drippings in the skillet. Increase the heat to medium-high and bring to a boil. Cook until reduced by one-half, stirring frequently. Reduce the heat to medium and stir in the madeira, parsley and tarragon. Whisk in 2 tablespoons butter, 1 tablespoon at a time. Cook until the sauce is slightly thickened. Add the chicken and cook for 1 minute or until heated through. Garnish with the capers and serve.

Curried Chicken and Cauliflower

Serves 6 to 8

Curry ingredients vary in many Asian countries. This freshly prepared version
will keep you from reaching for the curry powder in your kitchen.

> 2 tablespoons sesame seeds
> 2 tablespoons cumin seeds
> 3 garlic cloves
> 2 tablespoons grated fresh ginger
> 3 tablespoons dry roasted peanuts
> 3/4 teaspoon turmeric
> 1/2 teaspoon cinnamon
> 1 teaspoon salt
> 1/2 teaspoon cayenne pepper
> 1/2 cup unsweetened shredded coconut
> 1 cup (about) chicken broth
> 3/4 cup thinly sliced onions
> 3 tablespoons olive oil
> 1 pound boneless chicken breasts,
>   cut into 1 1/2-inch pieces
> 1 head cauliflower, cut into bite-size pieces
> Grated zest and juice of 1 lemon

Toast the sesame seeds and cumin seeds in a small skillet over medium heat, stirring constantly and watching carefully to prevent burning. Remove to a blender. Add the garlic, ginger, peanuts, turmeric, cinnamon, salt, cayenne pepper, coconut and 1/4 cup of the broth. Process until smooth, adding the remaining broth gradually.

Sauté the onions in the olive oil in a heavy saucepan over medium heat until light golden brown. Add the chicken and sauté until almost cooked through. Stir in the coconut mixture and cauliflower. Cook over low heat until the cauliflower is tender-crisp and the chicken is cooked through, stirring occasionally. Add additional broth if the sauce is too thick. Stir in the lemon zest and lemon juice and serve.

The Cincinnati Masters is an annual tennis event held in the Cincinnati suburb of Mason, Ohio. The event started on September 18, 1899, and today is the oldest tennis tournament in the United States that is played in its original city.

Chicken with Lemon and Olives

Serves 6

Influenced by the tagines in Morocco, this tasty dish uses many traditional ingredients and is easily prepared on the stove.

> 3 tablespoons olive oil
> 2 tablespoons unsalted butter
> 1 (3-pound) chicken, cut up
> 1 onion, thinly sliced
> 3 garlic cloves, crushed
> 3 tablespoons grated fresh ginger
> 2 teaspoons turmeric
> 1/2 teaspoon cayenne pepper
> 1/2 teaspoon cinnamon
> 2 cups chicken broth
> 1/2 cup niçoise olives
> 1/3 cup picholine olives
> 2 lemons
> Additional lemon juice to taste

Heat the olive oil and butter in a heavy saucepan. Add the chicken in batches and cook until brown on all sides. Remove the chicken with tongs to a plate. Add the onion to the drippings in the saucepan and sauté until translucent. Add the garlic and sauté for 3 minutes. Add the ginger, turmeric, cayenne pepper and cinnamon and sauté for 2 minutes. Return the chicken to the saucepan and stir in the broth. Simmer, covered, for 30 minutes. Add the olives and simmer for 30 minutes or until the chicken is tender and cooked through. Grate the zest from the lemons and set aside. Juice the lemons and add the juice to the chicken. Cook until heated through, stirring occasionally. Stir in the lemon zest. Adjust the seasonings to taste, adding additional lemon juice, if desired.

NOTE: *Serve this dish with couscous on the side. A crisp salad makes it a delightful dinner.*

Chicken with Spinach
Serves 6

16 ounces fresh spinach
Juice of 1 lemon
Nutmeg to taste
2 eggs
6 boneless skinless chicken breasts
1/2 cup bread crumbs
1 tablespoon butter
1 tablespoon olive oil
8 ounces fresh mushrooms, sliced
2 onions, sliced
1 tablespoon butter
1 tablespoon olive oil

Arrange the spinach on a heatproof serving platter. Sprinkle with the lemon juice and nutmeg. Beat the eggs in a shallow dish. Dip the chicken in the eggs and coat in the bread crumbs. Heat 1 tablespoon butter and 1 tablespoon olive oil in a skillet. Add the chicken and cook for 10 minutes or until golden brown on both sides and cooked through.

Arrange the chicken over the spinach and place in a warm oven. Sauté the mushrooms and onions in 1 tablespoon butter and 1 tablespoon olive oil in a skillet until the vegetables are tender. Spoon over the chicken and serve immediately.

The ten galleries in the Cincinnati Reds Hall of Fame and Museum at the Great American Ball Park contain historic baseball documents, memorabilia, and photographs, as well as interactive broadcasting and batting/pitching opportunities. There are special tributes to each of the seventy-five members of the Reds Hall of Fame.

Herb Garden Chicken

Serves 4

4 chicken breasts
1 tablespoon grated lemon zest
1/3 cup fresh lemon juice
2 tablespoons olive oil
1 teaspoon garlic salt
1 teaspoon pepper
1/3 cup chopped fresh parsley
1/3 cup chopped fresh basil
1/3 cup chopped fresh thyme

Place the chicken in a sealable plastic bag. Whisk the lemon zest, lemon juice, olive oil, garlic salt, pepper, parsley, basil and thyme in a bowl and pour over the chicken. Seal tightly and turn to coat. Marinate in the refrigerator for 30 minutes to 4 hours, turning occasionally. Preheat the grill to medium and lightly oil the grill rack.

Drain the chicken, discarding the marinade. Grill the chicken, with the cover closed, for 20 minutes or until light brown on the bottom. Turn the chicken over and grill, covered, for 10 to 15 minutes or until brown and cooked through.

NOTE: *Feel free to mix and match the three herbs based on what is growing in your garden. Potential alternatives may include oregano, sage, cilantro, or chives.*

Mrs. Reed Bartlett is arranging for a children's radio program,
"Books Bring Adventure," which was presented every Saturday morning over WKRC
and sponsored by Junior League of Cincinnati

Chicken Vegetable Risotto

Serves 4

3 tablespoons olive oil

2 shallots, minced

8 ounces sliced mushrooms

1 cup arborio rice

3 1/2 cups chicken broth, heated

1 1/2 cups chopped cooked chicken

1/4 cup reconstituted sun-dried tomatoes or oil-pack
    sun-dried tomatoes, drained

3 green onions, chopped

1/4 cup (or more) fresh parsley, finely chopped

1/4 cup (1/2 stick) unsalted butter, softened

2/3 cup (or more) grated Parmesan cheese

Salt and freshly ground pepper to taste

Heat the olive oil in a heavy saucepan over medium-high heat. Add the shallots and mushrooms and sauté for 5 to 6 minutes. Add the rice and sauté for 3 to 4 minutes. Reduce the heat to medium. Add the broth 1/2 cup at a time, cooking until the broth is almost completely absorbed after each addition and stirring constantly. Stir in the chicken, tomatoes, green onions and 1/4 cup parsley before the last addition of broth. Stir in the remaining 1/2 cup broth and cook until the broth is absorbed, stirring constantly. Remove from the heat and stir in the butter, 2/3 cup cheese, salt and pepper. Sprinkle with additional cheese and chopped parsley, if desired, and serve.

NOTE: *This recipe could easily be adapted with other ingredients to accommodate your own tastes. Try using other vegetables or shrimp instead of chicken. Preparing risotto takes some work, but the taste is well worth it—so rich and creamy!*

The Junior League of Cincinnati's Kids in the Kitchen is an opportunity for kids to have a fun, hands-on approach to learning about healthy eating and exercise.

Entrees

Whole Roasted Turkey with Herbed Butter

Serves 10 to 12

1 cup cider vinegar
1/2 cup apple butter
1 teaspoon salt
10 fresh sage leaves
Leaves of 6 sprigs of rosemary, finely chopped
10 sprigs of thyme, finely chopped
1 1/2 cups (3 sticks) salted butter, softened
1 (13-pound) turkey

Combine the vinegar, apple butter, salt and sage in a saucepan and mix well. Bring to a boil. Reduce the heat to medium-low when the mixture becomes fragrant and let simmer. Combine the rosemary, thyme and butter in a bowl and mix well. Preheat the oven to 325 degrees. Separate the skin from the meat of the turkey by pushing your hand under the skin. Spread the butter mixture under the skin over the entire turkey. Insert a palm-size amount of the butter mixture into the cavity. Spread any remaining butter mixture over the outside of the turkey.

Place the turkey on a rack in a roasting pan. Pour one-third of the vinegar mixture over the turkey. Roast the turkey for 2 1/2 to 3 hours, basting every hour with the vinegar mixture. The skin will become very brown. Cover with foil and roast for 30 minutes longer or until a meat thermometer inserted into the thickest portion registers 180 degrees. Remove the turkey to a platter and cover with foil. Let rest for 10 minutes or longer before carving.

NOTE: *Be sure to rub the butter under all parts of the skin. You want every part of the bird to have a lot of flavor. Always be sure to check the temperature of the turkey. Do not rely on the pre-inserted thermometers that come with the turkey. You want the internal temperature to be 180 degrees.*

This recipe is from
Chef Caitlyn MacEachen Steininger
of "Cooking with Caitlyn."

Cincinnati Seasoned

November Enchiladas

Serves 4 to 5

The rich colors and exotic spices of the season inspired this recipe.

1 red bell pepper, chopped

1 red onion, chopped

1 teaspoon minced fresh garlic

10 ounces fresh spinach

1 teaspoon dried thyme

1 teaspoon dried oregano

1 tablespoon olive oil

8 ounces cream cheese, softened

1 teaspoon cumin

1 teaspoon coriander

8 ounces cooked turkey breast, shredded

Salt and pepper to taste

8 to 10 (6-inch) flour or corn tortillas

1/2 cup (1 stick) butter, melted

1/2 cup red enchilada sauce

1/4 cup chopped cilantro

Sauté the bell pepper, onion, garlic, spinach, thyme and oregano in the olive oil in a large skillet over medium heat until the vegetables are tender. Add the cream cheese, cumin and coriander and cook until the cheese is melted, stirring constantly. Remove from the heat and stir in the turkey, salt and pepper. Preheat the oven to 350 degrees.

Brush both sides of the tortillas with the butter and lay on a work surface. Spoon equal portions of the chicken mixture onto the center of each tortilla and roll up. Arrange the rolled tortillas seam side down in a baking pan and brush with the enchilada sauce. Sprinkle with the cilantro. Bake, covered with foil, for 15 minutes. Serve immediately.

NOTE: *Feel free to use more or less melted butter, and be sure to have the tortillas at room temperature before filling.*

The Junior League of Cincinnati partnered with Girls on the Run Cincinnati for a two-year project targeting girls ages eight to eleven in lower-income schools. The League committed financial and logistical support as well as volunteer staffing.

Entrees

Kentucky Hot Brown Casserole

Serves 6

1/4 cup (1/2 stick) low-fat margarine

1/4 cup all-purpose flour

1 chicken bouillon cube

2 cups skim milk

6 slices wheat bread, toasted

1 pound thinly sliced or shredded
  cooked turkey

2/3 cup shredded low-fat Cheddar
  cheese or mozzarella cheese

2 tomatoes, sliced

6 slices bacon, crisp-cooked
  and crumbled

Preheat the oven to 350 degrees. Melt the margarine in a saucepan over low heat. Stir in the flour. Cook until smooth, stirring constantly. Stir in the bouillon cube and milk. Cook over medium heat for 5 minutes or until thick and bubbly, stirring constantly. Remove from the heat. Arrange the toast in a single layer in a 9×13-inch baking dish coated with nonstick cooking spray. Top each slice with the turkey and spoon the white sauce evenly over the top. Layer the cheese, tomatoes and bacon over the sauce. Bake for 20 to 25 minutes.

Citrus Ginger Salmon

Serves 2

2 tablespoons dark brown sugar

1 1/2 teaspoons grated fresh ginger

1 tablespoon Dijon mustard

1 tablespoon Asian fish sauce

1 tablespoon orange juice

1 pinch of coarse sea salt

2 salmon fillets

Freshly cracked pepper to taste

Preheat the broiler to high. Combine the brown sugar, ginger, Dijon mustard, fish sauce, orange juice and salt in a bowl and mix well. Sprinkle the flesh side of the salmon generously with pepper. Arrange the salmon skin side up on a broiler pan coated with nonstick cooking spray or olive oil. Broil 6 inches from the heat source for 3 minutes. Turn the fish over and coat the flesh side with the ginger mixture. Broil for 3 minutes or until the fish begins to flake.

Cincinnati Seasoned

Dijon and
Brown Sugar–Glazed Salmon

Serves 6

6 (4- to 6-ounce) salmon fillets (1 inch thick)

¹/4 cup extra-virgin olive oil

¹/4 cup light soy sauce

¹/4 cup Dijon mustard

3 tablespoons prepared mustard

2 tablespoons light brown sugar

1 teaspoon seasoned rice vinegar

Salt and pepper to taste

Place the salmon in a sealable plastic bag. Combine the olive oil, soy sauce, Dijon mustard, prepared mustard, brown sugar and vinegar in a bowl and whisk until blended. Remove and reserve ¹/3 cup of the marinade. Pour the remaining marinade over the salmon. Seal tightly and turn to coat. Marinate in the refrigerator for 15 to 30 minutes. Remove the salmon and discard the marinade. Season the salmon lightly with salt and pepper.

To grill the salmon, preheat the grill. Grill the salmon skin side down over indirect heat for 10 to 12 minutes or until the fish begins to flake, brushing with the reserved marinade during the last 2 minutes of cooking.

To broil the salmon, preheat the broiler. Arrange the salmon skin side down on a broiler pan coated with nonstick cooking spray. Broil for 5 minutes. Brush with the reserved marinade and broil for 3 to 5 minutes longer or until the fish begins to flake.

Popular local attraction Coney Island started in the 1870s as an apple orchard farm owned by James Parker, who realized that his location along the Ohio River was a profitable place to draw visitors. The Sunlite Pool at Coney Island is the largest recirculating swimming pool in the world.

Entrées

Sea Bass with Citrus Salsa

Serves 6

2 (11-ounce) cans mandarin oranges, drained and
    coarsely chopped
1/2 cup finely chopped red bell pepper
1/3 cup finely chopped red onion
1/4 cup honey mustard
1 tablespoon fresh lime juice
1 tablespoon chopped fresh cilantro
1/2 teaspoon cracked pepper
6 (8-ounce) sea bass fillets
1/4 teaspoon kosher salt
1/8 teaspoon garlic powder

Combine the oranges, bell pepper, onion, mustard, lime juice, cilantro and pepper in a bowl and mix well. Chill for several hours. Preheat the grill. Sprinkle the sea bass with equal portions of the salt and garlic powder. Grill the sea bass for 4 minutes per side or until the fish begins to flake. Remove to serving plates and top each fillet with 1/4 cup of the citrus salsa.

NOTE: *The salsa is also great with chicken, pork, or shrimp.*

Tuna Steaks with Capers and Oregano

Serves 4

1/4 cup capers, drained

2 tablespoons chopped fresh oregano

1/2 tablespoon extra-virgin olive oil

1 small shallot, minced

Salt and pepper to taste

4 (6-ounce) tuna steaks (3/4 inch thick)

1 tablespoon extra-virgin olive oil

4 anchovy fillets, chopped

1 cup dry red wine

2 tablespoons cold unsalted butter, cut into 2 pieces

Extra-virgin olive oil for drizzling

4 cups packed baby arugula

Combine the capers, oregano, 1/2 tablespoon olive oil, the shallot, salt and pepper in a small bowl and mix well. Season the tuna steaks with salt and pepper. Heat 1 tablespoon olive oil in a skillet over high heat until shimmering. Add the tuna and cook for 4 minutes or to medium-rare, turning once. Remove the tuna to a platter and keep warm.

Add the anchovies to the skillet and cook over medium heat for 1 minute or until dissolved, mashing with a fork while cooking. Stir in the wine. Cook until reduced by one-half, stirring occasionally. Remove from the heat. Stir in the butter and season with salt and pepper. Drizzle olive oil over the arugula in a bowl and season with salt.

Place one tuna steak on each of four serving plates and mound equal portions of the arugula next to the tuna. Pour the wine sauce over the tuna and top with the caper mixture.

Pan-Seared Sea Scallops with Pine Nut Vinaigrette, Spinach, Tomato and Artichoke Hearts

Serves 2

1/2 cup pine nuts
3 garlic cloves, roasted
1/4 cup vegetable stock
Salt and pepper to taste
4 large sea scallops
1 to 2 tablespoons olive oil
1/4 cup quartered artichoke hearts
1/4 cup chopped Roma tomato
2 cups baby spinach

Preheat the oven to 350 degrees. Spread the pine nuts in a shallow baking pan. Bake for 3 to 8 minutes or until golden brown. Remove to a wire rack and let cool. Process the cooled pine nuts, garlic, stock, salt and pepper in a blender until smooth.

Season the scallops with salt and pepper. Heat a skillet over high heat and pour in the olive oil. Add the scallops and cook for 1 to 2 minutes per side or until golden brown and tender. Remove the scallops to a plate and keep warm.

Add the artichokes and tomatoes to the skillet and sauté over medium heat for 1 minute. Add the spinach and sauté for 30 seconds or until wilted. Spoon the spinach mixture onto two serving plates. Top each with two scallops and serve the pine nut vinaigrette on the side.

This recipe is from
Executive Chef Blake J. Maier,
Vineyard Café & Wineroom.

Pan-Seared Scallops with White Wine Sauce

Serves 2

4 large sea scallops

Sea salt and crushed pepper to taste

2 tablespoons extra-virgin olive oil

2 tablespoons unsalted butter

1/4 cup sauvignon blanc or other white wine

Rinse the scallops and remove and discard the abductor muscle. Pat the scallops dry with a paper towel. Season one side of the scallops with salt and pepper. Heat a skillet over medium heat. Combine the olive oil and butter in the skillet and cook until the butter is melted.

Add the scallops seasoned side down. Season the top of the scallops with salt and pepper. Cook for 30 to 60 seconds and turn over. Cook for 30 to 60 seconds and remove from the heat. Add the wine to the skillet and return to the heat. Cook for 30 seconds and turn the scallops. Cook for 30 seconds longer. Remove the scallops to serving plates and drizzle with the wine sauce from the skillet.

Bargain Box was a signature Junior League of Cincinnati project that provided families an opportunity to buy necessary items for their homes and loved ones. The project worked through the generosity of League members, who donated thousands of gently used items. The League then distributed thousands of vouchers to area women's shelters and schools. The initiative allowed members of the community to discover a second life for many things including business suits, home appliances, furniture, and children's clothing.

Spicy Shrimp and Creamy Grits

Serves 6

GRITS

3 cups chicken stock

1 1/2 teaspoons salt

1/2 teaspoon white pepper

1 1/2 cups white grits

2 cups milk

1 cup heavy cream

6 tablespoons butter

1 cup (4 ounces) shredded white
　Cheddar cheese

1/2 cup (2 ounces) grated
　Parmesan cheese

SPICY SAUCE

1 1/2 tablespoons paprika

1 1/2 tablespoons black pepper

1 1/2 tablespoons onion powder

1 1/2 tablespoons oregano

1 tablespoon garlic powder

1 tablespoon cayenne pepper

2 teaspoons salt

1 green bell pepper, chopped

1 white onion, chopped

3 tablespoons olive oil

3 tablespoons all-purpose flour

1/4 cup white wine

1 tablespoon Worcestershire sauce

Juice of 1 lemon

1/2 cup heavy cream

Hot red pepper sauce to taste

SHRIMP

24 peeled fresh shrimp with tails

Salt and black pepper to taste

Cayenne pepper to taste

1/4 cup crisp-cooked pancetta
　for garnish

1/4 cup chopped flat-leaf parsley
　for garnish

1 lemon, sliced for garnish

For the grits, combine the chicken stock, salt and white pepper in a large saucepan and bring to a boil. Stir in the grits gradually and reduce the heat to low. Simmer for 45 minutes, stirring every 10 minutes without scraping the bottom of the pan. Gradually stir in the milk, cream and butter as the grits thicken. Fold in the Cheddar cheese and Parmesan cheese just before serving.

For the sauce, combine the paprika, 1 1/2 tablespoons black pepper, the onion powder, oregano, garlic powder, cayenne pepper and 2 teaspoons salt in a bowl and mix well. Sauté the bell pepper and onion in the olive oil in a saucepan over medium heat until translucent. Stir in the flour. Cook for a few minutes, stirring constantly. Reduce the heat to low and stir in the wine, Worcestershire sauce and spice mixture. Stir in the lemon juice, cream and hot sauce.

For the shrimp, season the shrimp with salt, black pepper and cayenne pepper. Cook the shrimp in a nonstick skillet over medium heat until the shrimp turn pink. Divide the grits between four serving plates and top with equal portions of the spicy sauce. Arrange four shrimp on top of each serving and garnish with the pancetta, parsley and lemon slices.

The grits should be started first since they take the longest to cook. Everything else can be done simultaneously while the grits are cooking. Grits should be the old-fashioned kind, preferably stone-ground. The instant variety should be avoided. Polenta can be substituted for grits. If using polenta, prepare according to the package directions, adding the cheese just before serving. There is a depth to the flavors in this dish that belie the fact that it only takes an hour to prepare. Serve with a sweeter wine to complement the spicy kick or a Kentucky bourbon mint julep on a cool spring day to prepare for the races. This dish will bring a taste of the South to Cincinnati and warm up any chilly day.

Cincinnati Seasoned

Caribbean–Spiced Grilled Shrimp

Serves 6

*Influenced by tropical island spices and fruit, this quick-cooking entrée
can also be served as a first course or an appetizer.*

2 pounds (11- to 15-count) jumbo fresh shrimp
2 serrano chiles, chopped
3/4 cup orange juice
1/2 cup pineapple juice
Juice of 1 lime
2 tablespoons grated fresh ginger
1/4 teaspoon ground allspice
2 garlic cloves, crushed
1 teaspoon olive oil
1 teaspoon salt

Peel and devein the shrimp, leaving the tails intact. Place the shrimp in a sealable plastic bag. Combine the chiles, orange juice, pineapple juice, lime juice, ginger, allspice, garlic, olive oil and salt in a bowl and mix well. Pour over the shrimp. Seal tightly and turn to coat. Marinate in the refrigerator for 8 hours to overnight, turning occasionally. Preheat the grill to medium. Drain the shrimp, reserving the marinade. Grill the shrimp for 2 minutes per side or until the shrimp turn pink, basting frequently with the reserved marinade; do not overcook. Discard any remaining marinade.

NOTE: *Adjust the heat of the dish by removing the seeds from the chiles to decrease the spiciness or adding cayenne pepper to taste to increase spiciness. Serve with your favorite fresh fruit salsa, grilled vegetables, and basmati rice for a delightful meal.*

Visit Cincinnati, and you will no doubt be treated to the tradition of Montgomery Inn. Family patriarch Ted Gregory opened the original restaurant in Montgomery in 1951. A former stagecoach stop, it was originally known as a place to enjoy beverages but not necessarily food. Ted would share his home-cooked meals with those who stopped by, and one day his wife, Matula, prepared barbecued ribs with homemade sauce, which were a hit. With the help of Matula and their children, preparing the ribs became a labor of love and a family tradition. Dubbed "The Ribs King" by a local journalist, Ted kept the name until his death in 2001. These days, the Montgomery Inn restaurants attract U.S. presidents, actors, entertainers, and astronauts.

Cincinnati Seasoned

Tart and Tangy Shrimp

Serves 4

1 pound peeled fresh shrimp

1/4 cup olive oil

2 tablespoons Paul Prudhomme's
   Blackened Redfish Magic

2 tablespoons honey

2 tablespoons chopped fresh parsley

1 tablespoon soy sauce

2 tablespoons lemon juice

Tabasco sauce to taste

Place the shrimp in a sealable plastic bag. Whisk the olive oil, redfish seasoning, honey, parsley, soy sauce, lemon juice and Tabasco sauce in a bowl and pour over the shrimp. Seal tightly and turn to coat. Marinate in the refrigerator for 4 hours or longer, turning occasionally. Preheat the oven to 350 degrees. Pour the shrimp and marinade into a 9×13-inch baking dish. Bake until the shrimp turn pink and the sauce is bubbly.

NOTE: *You may substitute Paul Prudhomme's Seafood Magic for the Redfish Magic if you prefer less spice.*

Shrimp, Asparagus and Cannellini Bean Penne

Serves 6

3 cups asparagus pieces

1 1/2 cups chopped onions

2 teaspoons minced garlic

1 tablespoon extra-virgin olive oil

1 cup sliced portobello mushrooms

12 ounces deveined peeled
   fresh shrimp

1/2 teaspoon shredded fresh basil

1/2 teaspoon dried red pepper flakes

1/2 cup dry white wine

3 tablespoons grated lemon zest

2 (14-ounce) cans cannellini
   beans, drained

Salt to taste

12 ounces penne, cooked, drained
   and kept warm

1/4 cup pine nuts, toasted

Sauté the asparagus, onions and garlic in the olive oil in a skillet for 5 minutes. Add the mushrooms, shrimp, basil and red pepper flakes and sauté for 5 minutes or until the shrimp turn pink. Stir in the wine and lemon zest.

Mash one-fourth of the beans in a bowl and add to the shrimp mixture. Stir in the remaining beans. Cook for 3 to 5 minutes or until heated through, stirring frequently. Season with salt. Serve over the pasta and sprinkle with the pine nuts.

Entrees

Carolina Carbonara

Serves 4

*There are many variations to carbonara in Italy. This version is best served
on a cold, blustery day because it's very thick and creamy.*

4 ounces bacon, chopped
6 tablespoons butter
1 cup milk
2 tablespoons white wine vinegar
16 ounces spaghetti
2 eggs, beaten
1/2 cup (2 ounces) grated Parmigiano-Reggiano cheese
1/4 cup white wine
1 small onion, chopped and cooked until caramelized
1 cup frozen peas
Salt and pepper to taste
Shredded Parmesan cheese

Cook the bacon in a small skillet until light brown; drain. Add the butter to
the skillet and cook the bacon until the butter becomes clear. Heat the milk in
saucepan until hot. Stir in the bacon with butter and the vinegar; the milk will
curdle. Cook for 15 minutes or until the milk mixture is smooth, stirring frequently.
Cook the pasta in a large saucepan of boiling water until al dente. Drain and
immediately return to the saucepan. Add the eggs, 1/2 cup cheese, wine, bacon
sauce, onion and peas and cook just until the eggs are set, tossing constantly. Season
with salt and pepper. Sprinkle with cheese.

NOTE: *You may add cooked chicken or shrimp to the dish. You may also substitute
prosciutto for the bacon.*

Baked Penne with Italian Sausage

Serves 8

2 teaspoons minced garlic
1 tablespoon olive oil
1 (6-ounce) can tomato paste
1 (28-ounce) can crushed tomatoes
1 tablespoon sugar
Salt and pepper to taste
15 ounces ricotta cheese
1 1/2 cups (6 ounces) shredded mozzarella cheese
8 ounces penne, cooked al dente, rinsed and drained
1 pound bulk Italian sausage, cooked, drained
    and crumbled
1 1/2 cups (6 ounces) shredded mozzarella cheese

Preheat the oven to 350 degrees. Sauté the garlic in the olive oil in a saucepan for 2 to 3 minutes. Add the tomato paste and cook for a few minutes, stirring constantly. Stir in the tomatoes, sugar, salt and pepper. Cook for a few minutes, stirring occasionally.

Mix the ricotta cheese and 1 1/2 cups mozzarella cheese in a bowl. Season with salt and pepper. Spread 1/2 cup of the tomato sauce over the bottom of an 8×11-inch baking dish. Layer one-half of the pasta, 1 cup of the tomato sauce, the ricotta mixture, sausage and 1 cup tomato sauce in the baking dish in the order listed. Top with the remaining pasta and tomato sauce. Sprinkle with 1 1/2 cups mozzarella cheese. Place the baking dish on a baking sheet. Bake for 35 minutes or until bubbly.

NOTE: *This dish can be made the day before and reheated. You may substitute chicken or ground beef for the sausage. Add roasted or sautéed vegetables for added flavor.*

The Cincinnati Reds franchise originated in 1882 as a charter member of the American Association. The name "Reds" was inspired by a previous, unrelated club called the Cincinnati Red Stockings, recognized as the first openly professional baseball team.

Cincinnati Seasoned

Fusilli Delicioso

Serves 8

*This is a deliciously light pasta. It's great for dinner parties
and serving a large number of people.*

1 pound bacon
2 tablespoons olive oil
4 garlic cloves, chopped
1 red onion, chopped
16 ounces fusilli
5 Roma tomatoes, chopped
16 ounces fresh spinach
4 ounces crumbled feta cheese
1/3 cup fresh basil, chopped
1/2 cup (2 ounces) freshly grated Parmesan cheese

Cook the bacon in the olive oil in a skillet until brown and crisp. Remove the bacon to a paper towel-lined plate. Crumble the bacon. Sauté the garlic and onion in the skillet until tender. Cook the fusillii in a large saucepan of boiling water until al dente. Drain and keep hot. Spread the tomatoes over the bottom of the hot saucepan and top with the spinach. Add the bacon and onion mixture. Top with the feta cheese and basil. Add the hot pasta and let stand for 2 minutes. Toss the mixture until the spinach begins to wilt. Sprinkle with the Parmesan cheese and serve.

NOTE: *Make sure all of your ingredients are chopped and prepared before you drain the fusilli. The pasta should be piping hot when it is poured on top of the other ingredients in order to wilt the spinach. The closer you can return it to the saucepan after it is finished cooking, the better! You may add shredded cooked chicken for a heartier dish.*

Cajun Cream Pasta

Serves 4

This recipe is the most popular pasta dish at Indigo Restaurant

1/4 cup (1/2 stick) butter
1 pound boneless skinless chicken
    breasts, cut into bite-size pieces
1 tablespoon chopped fresh garlic
1 (14-ounce) can artichoke hearts,
    drained and chopped
4 ounces black olives or
    kalamata olives

2 Roma tomatoes, chopped
2 tablespoons Cajun seasoning
2 cups heavy cream
2 tablespoons grated fresh
    Parmesan cheese
16 ounces dry pasta, or 2 pounds
    fresh pasta, cooked al dente,
    drained and kept warm

Melt the butter in a 14-inch skillet. Add the chicken and cook for 4 minutes per side. Stir in the garlic, artichokes, olives, tomatoes and Cajun seasoning. Stir in the cream and cheese. Bring to a boil and cook until reduced by one-third, stirring frequently. Add the pasta and toss to mix.

Homegrown Garden Pasta

Serves 2

*The hot zucchini and cool tomatoes make for a great combination
to celebrate your garden's summertime bounty.*

1 large zucchini, chopped
1 garlic clove, chopped
1 1/2 teaspoons extra-virgin olive oil
4 ounces linguini, cooked, drained
    and kept warm
1 1/2 teaspoons extra-virgin olive oil

1 large tomato, chopped
15 basil leaves, shredded
Sea salt and cracked black pepper
    to taste
2 tablespoons shredded
    Parmesan cheese

Sauté the zucchini and garlic in 1 1/2 teaspoons olive oil in a skillet over medium heat until the zucchini is tender. Add the pasta and drizzle with 1 1/2 teaspoons olive oil. Add the tomato, basil, salt and pepper and stir just until combined. Remove from the heat and serve sprinkled with the cheese.

NOTE: *Be sure to shred the basil to release the most oil from the leaves. Top with toasted pine nuts and add grilled chicken to add protein to this dish.*

Cincinnati Seasoned

Tuscan Sun Chicken Pasta

Serves 6

Your dinner guests will never know it only took about 20 minutes to prepare this bright, colorful, and flavorful dish.

3 cups fresh parsley
2 tablespoons fresh basil leaves
$1/2$ cup olive oil
4 garlic cloves
Coarse salt and freshly ground pepper to taste
1 (5-ounce) package sunflower kernels
1 cup chopped sun-dried tomatoes
$1/4$ cup olive oil
6 chicken breasts
16 ounces whole wheat linguini
1 cup (4 ounces) grated Parmesan cheese

Process the parsley, basil, $1/2$ cup olive oil, the garlic, salt and pepper in a blender or food processor until smooth. Remove to a bowl and stir in the sunflower kernels and tomatoes. Heat $1/4$ cup olive oil in a skillet. Add the chicken and cook for 12 minutes or until cooked through, turning occasionally. Remove to a plate and keep warm. Cook the pasta according to the package directions. Drain and remove to a large bowl. Pour the parsley mixture over the hot pasta and toss lightly to coat. Serve with the chicken and sprinkle with the cheese, salt and pepper.

NOTE: *If you are in a time crunch, you may use prepared pesto in place of the parsley, basil, $1/2$ cup olive oil, and garlic.*

Side Dishes

The Cincinnati Zoo and Botanical Garden

The Cincinnati Zoo and Botanical Garden, the second oldest zoo in the country, strives to, "inspire passion for nature and save wildlife for future generations," according to its mission statement. Judging from the visits made by more than 1.2 million people annually, the Zoo seems to be doing just that.

When it opened its doors in 1875, two years after the Zoological Society of Cincinnati was founded, the Zoo was home to few animals. The original collection included only two grizzly bears, three deer, six raccoons, eight monkeys, two elk, a buffalo, a hyena, a tiger, a circus elephant, an alligator and four hundred birds. Today the Zoo showcases more than five hundred animal specials and three thousand plant varieties, making it one of the largest collections in the country. Not only that, it is consistently distinguished by peer zoological parks as one of the top facilities in the nation. It is no surprise to find the Zoo's many parking lots full on any given day, any time of the year.

One of the Zoo's crown jewels is the Elephant House, which was constructed in 1906. A national historic landmark, the Taj Mahal-like structure is one of the most popular sites at the Zoo and was once though of as the "center of Cincinnati" because of

its precise location at the heart of Cincinnati's many neighborhoods.

The Zoo delights members and guests alike with a variety of special programs, starting at the beginning of the year with the conclusion of the popular Festival of Lights. Zoo Blooms boasts a canvas of color to celebrate spring with one of the Midwest's largest tulip displays, including more than 80,000 tulips and over a million daffodils, flowering shrubs and trees, hyacinths, and other spring bulbs. Zoo Babies amazes both children and adults with the Zoo's newest arrivals. Painted storks throughout the park show the way to the cutest and furriest, and visitors can learn about them in "Baby Talks," given by Zoo staff. The theme for Zoofari, the Zoo's premier fund-raising gala, is always a thrilling surprise. And, what is a better place to trick-or-treat than amongst the animals for three weeks of HallZOOeen? Not to be forgotten are the beloved Zoo summer camps for all ages and the WILD nights of the Zoo's overnight slumber parties for children age five and older.

Visit www.cincinnatizoo.org to plan your next trip to the place where the wild things are!

Little One's Birthday Party

Healthy Tropical Fruit Smoothie

———

Pepperoni Pizza Dip

Chocolate Zucchini Muffins

Baked Penne with Italian Sausage

———

Cowboy Cookies

Tuxedo Ice Cream Cake

Asparagus with Pecans

Serves 4

1¹/2 pounds small asparagus spears	*¹/4 cup sugar*
2 tablespoons vegetable oil	*³/4 cup chopped pecans*
¹/4 cup cider vinegar	*Pepper to taste*
¹/4 cup soy sauce	

Cook the asparagus in a saucepan of boiling water for 6 to 7 minutes or until tender-crisp and bright green. Drain and rinse with cold water. Arrange the asparagus in one or two layers in an oblong dish. Whisk the oil, vinegar, soy sauce and sugar in a bowl. Stir in the pecans. Pour over the asparagus, moving the spears to be certain the liquid reaches all of the asparagus. Sprinkle with pepper and serve.

Sautéed Green Beans

Serves 4

2 tablespoons butter or margarine	*1 cup water*
Olive oil (optional)	*Black pepper to taste*
1 pound green beans, trimmed and	*Lemon pepper to taste*
cut into bite-size pieces	*Salt to taste*
1 garlic clove, crushed	*Goya Adobo without Pepper to taste*

Melt the butter in a nonstick skillet over medium heat. Add olive oil if necessary to cover the bottom of the skillet. Add the beans and garlic and sauté until the garlic is golden brown. Add the water, black pepper, lemon pepper and salt and cook until the beans are tender. Remove the beans with a slotted spoon to a serving dish. Season with Adobo and serve warm.

NOTE: *Goya Adobo is a seasoning mix found in the Hispanic section at the grocery store.*

Beginning in 2000, the Junior League of Cincinnati spent two years researching different ways the League could work within their focus area: strengthening childhood environments. The League's research ultimately uncovered a critical gap in services for children in the area of mental health. Recognizing this need, the Junior League of Cincinnati outlined its goals for a five-year collaborative initiative called MindPeace. Working in conjunction with Cincinnati Children's Hospital Medical Center and more than thirty other community organizations, MindPeace has received many honors including the Community Activist Award from the Division of Psychiatry at Cincinnati Foundation and the Junior League Award for Collaboration.

Buttered Haricots Vert

Serves 8 to 12

Kosher salt to taste
3 pounds haricots vert (French green beans),
stem ends trimmed
1 to 2 tablespoons butter
Freshly ground pepper to taste
1/4 cup water
1 tablespoon minced shallot (optional)
1 tablespoon chopped dill weed (optional)
1 tablespoon grated lemon zest (optional)

Bring a large saucepan of generously salted water to a boil over medium-high heat. Add the beans and cook for 3 minutes. Drain and let cool. Arrange the beans in a glass or ceramic baking dish. Dot with the butter and season with salt and pepper. Add 1/4 cup water and the shallot. Cover with plastic wrap and chill overnight.

Preheat the oven to 350 degrees. Remove the plastic wrap and cover the baking dish with foil. Bake for 15 minutes or until heated through. Remove the beans to a serving platter and sprinkle with the dill weed and lemon zest.

NOTE: *These could be made the evening of a party if you boil the green beans just until tender, then toss with the butter and serve. On the day of the party, when time is short, use this 'caterer's cheating' variation, which keeps the stove and your hands free for the most part.*

This recipe is from
Chef Renée Schuler of
Eat Well.

The Junior League of Cincinnati made a two-year commitment to support Girls on the Run, a nonprofit program that encourages preteen girls to develop self-respect and healthy lifestyles through running. The curricula address all aspects of girls' development—physical, emotional, mental, social, and spiritual well-being.

Rajmah
(Indian Red Beans and Rice)

Serves 2 to 4

Great alone or served with greens for a vegetarian meal, this Indian favorite also makes a fantastic side dish to a chicken entrée.

1 russet potato, peeled

2 cups water

1 cup jasmine rice or favorite rice

1 tablespoon olive oil

1 white onion, chopped

1 (15-ounce) can kidney beans,
    rinsed and drained

1/2 teaspoon mustard seeds

5 teaspoons coriander

1 teaspoon turmeric

2 teaspoons chili powder

2 teaspoons salt

Cook the potato in a saucepan of boiling water until tender; drain. Mash the potato slightly and set aside. Bring 2 cups water to a boil in a saucepan and add the rice. Reduce the heat and simmer for 15 minutes. Remove from the heat and let stand, covered, for 5 minutes. Heat the olive oil in a skillet over medium heat. Add the onion and sauté until translucent. Stir in the potato, kidney beans, mustard seeds, coriander, turmeric, chili powder and salt. Cook over low heat until heated through, stirring occasionally. Fluff the rice with a fork and spoon into serving bowls. Top with the kidney bean mixture and serve.

NOTE: *Feel free to add one chopped tomato to up the ante when serving rajmah as a main entrée. A dash of hot sauce will also spice up the dish for those who like it hotter!*

Side Dishes

Broccoli and Cauliflower with Garlic and Ginger

Serves 6

3 tablespoons extra-virgin olive oil
1 pound fresh broccoli, cut into florets
1 1/4 pounds fresh cauliflower, cut into florets
Salt to taste
3/4 cup water
2 tablespoons extra-virgin olive oil
1 small red onion, chopped
Large pinch of crushed red pepper flakes
Crumbled saffron threads to taste
1/2 teaspoon yellow mustard seeds
1/2 teaspoon brown mustard seeds
4 garlic cloves, finely chopped
1 tablespoon finely chopped fresh ginger
1/3 cup chopped cilantro
1 lime, cut into wedges for garnish

Heat 3 tablespoons olive oil in a large skillet over medium-high heat. Add the broccoli, cauliflower, salt and water and reduce the heat to medium. Sauté for 8 to 10 minutes or until the vegetables are tender-crisp. Remove the vegetables to a large bowl.

Heat 2 tablespoons olive oil with the drippings in the skillet. Add the onion, red pepper flakes, saffron and salt. Sauté until the onion is golden brown. Add the yellow mustard seeds and brown mustard seeds and let sizzle for 1 minute. Add the garlic and ginger and sauté for 1 minute. Add the broccoli and cauliflower and sauté for 2 minutes. Season with salt. Sprinkle with the cilantro. Garnish with the lime wedges and serve.

Honey-Roasted Carrot Purée

Serves 8 to 10

Your guests won't believe that these are carrots!

4 pounds organic whole carrots
3 tablespoons canola oil
Kosher salt and freshly ground pepper to taste
3 tablespoons honey, or to taste
1/4 cup (1/2 stick) butter, softened
Thyme sprigs or rosemary sprigs for garnish

Preheat the oven to 350 degrees. Peel the carrots and cut into 2-inch pieces. Combine the carrots, canola oil, salt and pepper in a bowl and toss to coat. Spread the carrots over the bottom of a shallow baking pan. Bake for 45 to 60 minutes or until tender and brown. Remove the carrots to a food processor. Process for 5 minutes or until smooth. Add the honey and butter gradually, processing constantly until smooth. Adjust the seasonings to taste. Remove to a serving bowl and garnish with thyme sprigs.

NOTE: *This can be made one day ahead and chilled. Reheat in an ovenproof dish at 350 degrees for 1 hour, stirring once or twice during heating.*

This recipe is from
Chef Renée Schuler of
Eat Well.

Cincinnati was founded in 1788 by John Cleves Symmes and Colonel Robert Patterson. Cincinnati began as three settlements between the Little Miami and Great Miami rivers on the north shore of the Ohio River.

Summer Corn and Zucchini

Serves 4

2 ears fresh corn, husks removed
1 zucchini, chopped
1 tablespoon extra-virgin olive oil
1/2 Vidalia onion, chopped
1 garlic clove, minced
1 tablespoon minced fresh basil
Salt and pepper to taste
2 tablespoons shredded Parmesan cheese

Grill the corn over hot coals until tender. Cut the kernels from the ears with a sharp knife. Sauté the zucchini in the olive oil in a skillet until tender. Stir in the corn kernels, onion, garlic, basil, salt and pepper and cook until heated through. Sprinkle with the cheese and serve immediately.

Did you know Junior League of Cincinnati's Columbia Center was once the home of the Columbia Auction Gallery? Buyers from all over the tri-state area would arrive to take a gander at its first-floor bidding hall. That's when the Columbia Parkway entrance was turned into an grand picture window, and interested bidders stepped through ten-foot-high wooden doors on the side of the building.

Grilled Eggplant Roll–Ups

Serves 4

1 to 2 tablespoons salt
1 eggplant, peeled and cut into 8 (^{1}/4-inch) slices
2 tablespoons olive oil
^{1}/2 cup double concentrated Italian tomato paste
Italian seasoning
Salt and pepper to taste
4 ounces Parmesan cheese, shredded
8 ounces fresh mozzarella cheese, cut into 8 thin
*   long slices*
2 cups marinara sauce
Additional shredded Parmesan cheese

Dissolve the salt in a bowl of cold water. Add the eggplant slices and soak for 1 to 2 hours to reduce the bitterness. Drain the eggplant and pat dry with a paper towel. Preheat the grill to 350 degrees.

Arrange the eggplant in a shallow baking pan and drizzle with the olive oil. Grill the eggplant until tender and light brown on both sides. Remove to a work surface. Preheat the oven to 350 degrees. Spread equal portions of the tomato paste over the eggplant slices. Top each slice with 2 dashes Italian seasoning, salt and pepper to taste. Sprinkle evenly with 4 ounces Parmesan cheese. Top each with a slice of mozzarella cheese and roll up, securing with a wooden pick if needed. Arrange the roll-ups in an 8×11-inch baking pan and top evenly with the marinara sauce. Sprinkle with additional Parmesan cheese. Bake for 20 minutes or until heated through and the cheese is melted. Serve warm.

Cincinnati Seasoned

Cheddar Potato Bake
Serves 6 to 8

This side dish is a perfect complement to serve with steak, chicken, or pork.
It is easy to make and always a hit with guests when entertaining!

6 potatoes
$1/2$ cup (1 stick) butter
2 cups (8 ounces) shredded
    Cheddar cheese
$1^1/2$ cups sour cream

$1/3$ cup chopped onion
1 tablespoon salt, or to taste
$1/4$ teaspoon pepper
Paprika

Preheat the oven to 350 degrees. Cook the whole potatoes in a saucepan of boiling water until tender; drain. Shred the potatoes when cool. Cook the butter and cheese in a saucepan over low heat until the cheese is melted, stirring frequently. Combine the sour cream, onion, salt and pepper in a bowl and mix well. Stir in the cheese mixture. Fold in the potatoes. Spoon into a greased baking dish and sprinkle with paprika. Bake for 30 minutes.

NOTE: *If you run short on time and need to "cheat," you can use 6 to 7 servings of frozen mashed potatoes.*

Thanksgiving Sweet Potatoes
Serves 8

6 sweet potatoes, peeled and
    cut into halves
Dash of salt
$3/4$ cup half-and-half
$1/2$ cup (1 stick) butter

$1^1/2$ cups packed brown sugar
$1/4$ teaspoon nutmeg
$1/4$ teaspoon cinnamon
$1/4$ teaspoon ground allspice

Bring a large saucepan of water to a boil. Add the sweet potatoes and salt. Boil for 10 to 15 minutes or until the sweet potatoes are tender; drain. Add the half-and-half, butter, brown sugar, nutmeg, cinnamon and allspice. Cook over low heat until the butter is melted, stirring constantly.

NOTE: *You may use an immersion blender instead of stirring if you prefer a more creamy consistency.*

Korean–Style Spinach
Serves 4 to 6

2 tablespoons sesame oil
2 garlic cloves, minced
1/2 teaspoon red pepper flakes
1 tablespoon tamari or reduced-sodium soy sauce
1 teaspoon brown sugar
8 cups fresh spinach, rinsed well and still damp
1 tablespoon sesame seeds

Heat the sesame oil in a skillet over medium heat. Add the garlic, red pepper flakes, tamari and brown sugar and sauté for 30 seconds. Add the spinach and cook until wilted, tossing constantly. Remove from the heat and sprinkle with the sesame seeds. Serve hot, cold or at room temperature.

This recipe is from
Cincinnati-based
www.sparkrecipes.com.

Ricotta Spinach Bake
Serves 6 to 8

1 tablespoon finely chopped yellow onion
2 teaspoons all-purpose flour
1/2 teaspoon salt
1/2 teaspoon dry mustard
6 eggs, beaten
1 1/2 cups ricotta cheese
16 ounces fresh spinach, chopped, cooked
  and well drained
Fresh parsley for garnish

Preheat the oven to 350 degrees. Mix the onion, flour, salt and mustard in a bowl. Add the eggs and mix well. Stir in the cheese. Add the spinach and mix well. Spoon into a greased shallow 2-quart baking dish. Bake for 30 to 35 minutes or until a knife inserted near the center comes out clean. Garnish with fresh parsley and serve.

Cincinnati Seasoned

Zucchini with Dilled Cream Sauce
Serves 4

1 small onion, chopped
1 garlic clove, minced
2 tablespoons butter
3 zucchini, peeled and julienned
1 cup sour cream, at room temperature
2 tablespoons all-purpose flour
2 tablespoons chopped fresh dill weed
2 tablespoons vinegar

Sauté the onion and garlic in the butter in a skillet until tender. Add the zucchini and sauté until the zucchini is tender. Mix the sour cream and flour in a small bowl and spoon over the zucchini. Stir in the dill weed and vinegar. Simmer for 15 minutes.

Sautéed Zucchini and Mushrooms
Serves 6

1 zucchini
2 tablespoons extra-virgin olive oil
8 ounces mushrooms, sliced
1/2 teaspoon herbes de Provence or
*   Italian sesasoning*
Dash of salt
Dash of pepper

Cut the zicchini into halves lengthwise; slice crosswise. Heat the olive oil in a nonstick skillet until hot. Add the zucchini and mushrooms and sauté for 3 minutes. Add the herbes de Provence, salt and pepper and sauté for 2 minutes or until the vegetables are tender.

NOTE: *Herbes de Provence is a mixture which contains thyme, rosemary, basil, marjoram, bay leaf, and sometimes lavender.*

Orzo with Roasted Vegetables
Serves 4

1 1/2 cups chopped yellow summer squash
1 cup chopped onion
1 1/2 cups chopped Roma tomatoes
3 garlic cloves, thinly sliced
Leaves of 1 sprig of rosemary
2 tablespoons extra-virgin olive oil
1 tablespoon balsamic vinegar
Salt and pepper to taste
1 cup orzo, cooked, drained and kept warm
2 tablespoons extra-virgin olive oil
Juice of 1 lime

Preheat the oven to 425 degrees. Combine the squash, onion, tomato, garlic, rosemary, 2 tablespoons olive oil, the vinegar, salt and pepper in a large bowl and toss to coat. Spread the vegetables in a shallow baking pan. Bake for 20 minutes, stirring halfway through baking.

Let the vegetables cool slightly and remove to a large bowl. Add the orzo and toss to mix. Add 2 tablespoons olive oil, the lime juice and pepper and toss to coat. Serve hot, at room temperature or chilled.

NOTE: *This recipe works well with whatever vegetables you have on hand or whatever is in season.*

Orzo Florentine

Serves 6

16 ounces orzo
12 cups chicken broth
1 tablespoon olive oil
1 bunch spinach, stemmed and julienned
1 bunch green onions, chopped
Handful of fresh basil, chopped
3/4 cup crumbled feta cheese
1/2 cup pine nuts, toasted
1/4 cup olive oil
1/4 cup lemon juice
Salt and pepper to taste

Cook the orzo according to the package directions, using the chicken broth instead of water; drain. Mix the hot orzo and 1 tablespoon olive oil in a large bowl and let cool. Combine the spinach, green onions, basil, cheese and pine nuts in a bowl and toss to mix. Add to the cooled orzo and toss to mix.

Whisk 1/4 cup olive and the lemon juice in a small bowl. Add to the orzo mixture and toss to coat. Season with salt and pepper. Serve at room temperature or chilled.

Bratwurst? Strudel anyone? How about a Chicken Dance? Started in 1976 to showcase Cincinnati's rich German heritage, Oktoberfest-Zinzinnati's outdoor fall festival is now second only to the original Oktoberfest in Munich, Germany. German music, food, dance, and drink are enjoyed by more than 500,000 in the Queen City starting the third full weekend of September. Why Oktoberfest in September? The original Oktoberfest was that same weekend back in 1810 to celebrate a royal wedding in Germany. In keeping with Munich's tradition, we celebrate then, too.

Mrs. Thomas Campion, editor of the Junior League's monthly pamphlet

Creamy Polenta

Serves 2

2 cups chicken broth or chicken stock
1 cup polenta
1 cup chicken broth or chicken stock
1/2 cup (2 ounces) shredded Parmesan cheese
1/2 cup heavy cream

Bring 2 cups broth to a boil in a saucepan. Whisk in the polenta and reduce the heat to low. Cook until all of the liquid is absorbed, whisking constantly. Add 1 cup broth, the cheese and cream and cook until the cheese is melted, whisking constantly. Serve immediately.

NOTE: *If the cooked polenta sits too long before serving and becomes stiff, add up to 1 cup of additional broth and cook over medium-high heat until the liquid is absorbed, whisking constantly. Spread leftover polenta on a greased baking sheet and let stand for a few hours. Cut into shapes, dredge in flour, and fry in hot oil in a skillet. Delicious!*

This recipe is from
Chef Caitlyn MacEachen Steininger
of "Cooking with Caitlyn."

The Junior League was first founded in 1901 by Mary Harriman in New York City. The Association of Junior Leagues was formed twenty years later. By 1969, there were more than two hundred leagues across the country.

Wild Rice and Mushroom Pilaf

Serves 6

1 cup dried porcini or dried shiitake mushrooms,
stems removed
1 cup boiling water
1 cup wild rice, rinsed
1/2 cup fresh orange juice
1/4 cup dry sherry
1/2 cup sliced carrots
2 tablespoons chopped fresh parsley
Sea salt or soy sauce to taste
1/2 cup finely chopped walnuts or pecans

Cover the mushrooms with the boiling water in a heatproof bowl. Let soak for 30 minutes or until the mushrooms are softened. Drain the mushrooms through a wire mesh strainer into a 4-cup measuring cup. Add enough water to the mushroom liquid to measure 2 1/2 cups. Chop the mushrooms and set aside. Pour the mushroom liquid into a saucepan, discarding any sediment. Add the rice, orange juice, sherry and carrots. Bring to a boil. Reduce the heat and simmer, covered, for 30 minutes. Stir in the mushrooms. Cook until the rice is tender. Stir in the parsley, salt and nuts.

Rhubarb Chutney

Makes about 3 cups

1 pound rhubarb, coarsely chopped
8 ounces pitted dates, coarsely chopped
1 cup sugar
8 ounces sultana raisins
1 large onion, coarsely chopped
2 cups vinegar
1 teaspoon ginger
1/2 teaspoon cayenne pepper

Combine the rhubarb, dates, sugar, raisins, onion, vinegar, ginger and cayenne pepper in a saucepan. Cook until thickened and chunky, stirring frequently. Spoon into freezer containers when cool. Freeze for up to 3 months.

Horseradish Sauce

Makes 2 cups

2 cups plain yogurt
1/2 cup grated peeled fresh horseradish
2 tablespoons white wine vinegar
1 tablespoon Dijon mustard
1 teaspoon minced garlic
1 tablespoon fresh lemon juice
1/4 teaspoon salt

Drain the yogurt through a fine mesh sieve. Combine the yogurt, horseradish, vinegar, Dijon mustard, garlic, lemon juice and salt in a blender; process until well combined. Chill for up to 1 day. Serve with beef.

NOTE: *Wear rubber gloves and have good ventilation when peeling and grating fresh horseradish.*

Serrano Lime Mayo

Makes about 2³/4 cups

2 limes
1/2 bunch fresh chives, chopped
2 serrano chiles, seeded and minced
2 cups mayonnaise
1/2 cup sour cream
Salt and pepper to taste

Grate the zest from both limes and juice one lime. Combine the lime zest, lime juice, chives, chiles, mayonnaise and sour cream in a food processor and pulse to mix well. Season with salt and pepper.

Desserts

Fountain Square

The iconic symbol of Downtown Cincinnati is the historic Fountain Square. Erected in 1871 on the former site of a butcher's market, the Tyler Davidson Fountain was donated by Henry Probasco in memory of his brother-in-law, Tyler Davidson. This gift to the people of Cincinnati has remained a gathering spot for Cincinnatians for many years. City planners have redesigned and restored Fountain Square many times in its history, but one thing continues to remain the same—the square is the heart of Cincinnati.

After promising a beautiful centerpiece celebrating the Queen City, Probasco traveled to Munich, Germany, to commission a bronze allegorical fountain made by Ferdinand von Mueller and based on a design by Alexander von Kreling. Centered around "The Genius of Water," its vivid imagery represents the uses of water, both natural and man-made, with narrative reliefs and charming individual figures. To this day, people can still drink water from the four fountains circling the bronze centerpiece. The flowing streams feature fresh, non-chlorinated water.

In 1971 the Square was redesigned by the firm of RTKL, Baltimore, Maryland. The fountain was moved slightly and redirected to the west, and the size of the square's plaza was enlarged to reflect that of new buildings around it. The fountain was cleaned, restored, and rededicated in 2000. Six years later, the fountain was moved again to revitalize the city and positioned to reclaim its place as the center of the downtown district.

Fountain Square is the gathering place of the City of Cincinnati. On any given day, there are a variety of events happening on the square. Concerts and festivals lighten up the fountain, and Cincinnatians gather around the bronze beauty daily to enjoy a lunch and the square's amenities, including free Wi-Fi. During the coldest months, the square turns in to a winter wonderland with ice skating and winter activities. The fountain is a historical landmark that will be enjoyed for many years to come.

You can discover this classic symbol of Cincinnati by visiting www.myfountainsquare.com.

Valentine's Night for Two

Chocolate Raspberry Martinis

———

Miniature Goat Cheese Peppers

Fresh Spinach Salad

———

Carolina Carbonara

———

Rich and Sinful Chocolate Cake & Icing

Butterscotch and Toffee Trifle

Serves 12 to 16

A delightful spin on the classic English dessert.

4 eggs

2/3 cup packed dark brown sugar

2 1/2 tablespoons good-quality
    vanilla extract

2 tablespoons good-quality scotch

1/4 teaspoon salt

2 tablespoons cornstarch

1/4 cup heavy cream

2 cups milk

3/4 cup heavy cream

2/3 cup Irish cream liqueur

1/2 cup brewed coffee, chilled

2 (9-inch) layers devil's food cake,
    cut into cubes

2 cups toffee bits

3 cups heavy whipping cream

1/4 cup confectioners' sugar

Whisk the eggs, brown sugar, vanilla, scotch and salt in a bowl. Mix the cornstarch and 1/4 cup cream in a small bowl. Bring the milk and 3/4 cup cream to a simmer in a saucepan over medium heat. Stir in the cornstarch mixture and remove from the heat. Whisk one-third of the hot milk gradually into the egg mixture; whisk the egg mixture into the hot milk. Return to the heat and cook until thickened, whisking constantly. Pour the hot butterscotch filling through a fine mesh strainer into a bowl, discarding any lumps in the strainer. Chill in an ice bath or refrigerator until cold.

Mix the liqueur and coffee in a bowl. Spread one-half of the cake cubes in a glass serving bowl. Drizzle with one-half of the coffee mixture and top with one-third of the toffee bits. Repeat the layers. Chill for 4 hours to overnight. Beat 3 cups whipping cream and the confectioners' sugar in a mixing bowl until soft peaks form. Spread over the trifle and sprinkle with the remaining toffee bits. Serve immediately.

NOTE: *Trifles are fantastic for crowds because they improve if they are kept overnight, they look impressive layered in a glass bowl, and they feed many. Just before serving, add the final topping of whipped cream. For an updated presentation, use martini glasses, champagne flutes, or jelly jar glasses and make individual trifles—just make sure to clear out a shelf in the fridge.*

This recipe is from
Chef Renée Schuler of
Eat Well.

Chocolate Raspberry Truffle Cheesecake

Serves 16

1 1/2 cups graham cracker crumbs

2 tablespoons butter, melted

1 dash of cinnamon

2 tablespoons brown sugar

32 ounces cream cheese, softened

1/2 cup granulated sugar

4 eggs

1 teaspoon vanilla extract

1 tablespoon cornstarch

8 ounces cream cheese, softened

1 cup (6 ounces) semisweet chocolate chips, melted

1 cup fresh raspberries

Preheat the oven to 350 degrees. Combine the graham cracker crumbs and melted butter in a bowl and mix well. Stir in the cinnamon and brown sugar. Press firmly in a nonstick 9-inch springform pan. Bake for 10 minutes. Remove to a wire rack to cool. Reduce the oven temperature to 325 degrees. Beat 32 ounces cream cheese in a mixing bowl until light and fluffy. Beat in the granulated sugar slowly. Add the eggs one at a time, beating well after each addition. Beat in the vanilla and cornstarch. Pour over the cooled crust.

Combine 8 ounces cream cheese and the melted chocolate chips in a bowl and mix well. Spoon some of the chocolate mixture over one raspberry to cover completely and submerge the covered raspberry into the batter in the pan. Repeat with the remaining raspberries. Bake for 60 to 65 minutes or until the edge is set and the center jiggles slightly when moved. Remove to a wire rack to cool completely. Chill for 6 hours. Loosen from the side of the pan with a sharp knife and remove the side. Serve chilled.

Chocolate Chip Cheesecake

Serves 12 to 16

You will be impressed with yourself when you prepare this sophisticated but simple recipe because it tastes like it just came from the bakery!

16 ounces cream cheese, softened

1 cup sugar

2 cups sour cream

3 eggs

1 tablespoon vanilla extract

1¹/2 cups (9 ounces) semisweet chocolate chips

2 (9-inch) graham cracker or chocolate cookie pie shells

Preheat the oven to 350 degrees. Beat the cream cheese in a mixing bowl until light and fluffy. Beat in the sugar and sour cream. Beat in the eggs and vanilla. Stir in 1 cup of the chocolate chips.

Divide equally between the two pie shells and smooth the tops with a spatula. Sprinkle the remaining chocolate chips equally over the tops. Bake for 40 minutes. Turn off the heat and do not open the oven door for 1 hour. Remove to a wire rack to cool. Chill for 3 to 4 hours or until firm before serving.

In the late 1800s Thomas and Nicolas Aglamesis left their home in Greece and settled in Cincinnati. The brothers learned the ice cream trade and opened up their first ice cream parlor, The Metropolitan, in Norwood in 1908. Five years later the second location was built in Oakley, which in 1922 also included an ice cream plant with modern cooling machinery. During the Depression their business became known as the Algamesis Brothers. Retaining the Old World formulas as well as the tried-and-true methods of ice cream and candy manufacturing, Thomas's son, James T. Aglamesis, took over the business after his uncle's death. Today there is a third generation of Aglamesis family members that work with Jim to carry on the tradition that Cincinnatians have come to know and love.

Ice Cream Bombe

Serves 6

2 pints peach sorbet
1¹/₂ pints strawberry sorbet
1 pint vanilla ice cream or vanilla frozen yogurt
Fresh fruit for garnish

Freeze an 8-inch bowl in the freezer. Soften the peach sorbet and spread over the bottom of the frozen bowl. Cover with plastic wrap and freeze for 30 minutes; remove the plastic wrap. Soften the strawberry sorbet and spread evenly over the peach sorbet. Cover with plastic wrap and freeze for 30 minutes; remove the plastic wrap. Soften the ice cream and spread evenly over the strawberry sorbet. Cover with plastic wrap and freeze until firm; remove the plastic wrap. Dip the bowl briefly in warm water and run a sharp knife around the edge of the bowl to loosen. Invert immediately onto a serving plate. Cut into wedges and serve garnished with fresh fruit.

NOTE: *Feel free to use any combination of sorbet and ice cream flavors.*

Tuxedo Ice Cream Cake

Serves 15

24 chocolate sandwich cookies, crushed
1/2 cup (1 stick) margarine, melted
1/2 gallon vanilla ice cream, softened
2/3 cup evaporated milk
1/8 teaspoon salt
1/2 cup (1 stick) margarine
4 ounces German's sweet chocolate
1/3 cup sugar
1 teaspoon vanilla extract
8 ounces whipped topping

Spread the crushed cookies over the bottom of a greased 9×13-inch dish and drizzle with 1/2 cup melted margarine. Freeze until firm. Spread the softened ice cream evenly over the crust and freeze until firm.

Combine the evaporated milk, salt, 1/2 cup margarine, the chocolate, sugar and vanilla in a saucepan and bring to a boil. Cook for 4 minutes, whisking constantly. Remove from the heat and let cool. Pour evenly over the ice cream layer and freeze until firm. Spread the whipped topping over the chocolate layer and let stand for 10 to 15 minutes before serving.

The Museum Center conglomeration at the seventy-five-year-old Union Terminal houses the Cincinnati History Museum, Duke Energy Children's Museum, the Museum of Natural History and Science, and the Omnimax Theater. There truly is something interesting for everyone at one of the museums or special exhibits. The building was originally built as a unified terminal for multiple railroads passing through Cincinnati.

Peppermint Chocolate Icebox Cake

Serves 12

This is an easy recipe that's very pretty on the plate. It's a unique, decadent alternative to serve during the holiday season.

> 3 cups heavy whipping cream
> 3 tablespoons sugar
> 1 tablespoon peppermint extract
> 3 drops of red food coloring
> 2 boxes Anna's Chocolate Mint Thins cookies
> 10 peppermint candies, crushed
> 2 tablespoons chocolate syrup

Beat the whipping cream, sugar, peppermint extract and food coloring in a mixing bowl at high speed until soft peaks form. Arrange six cookies in a circle on a serving plate and place one cookie in the center. Spread 1/2 cup of the whipped cream over the cookies, leaving the edges of the cookies exposed. Repeat the layers to use all of the cookies. Spread the remaining whipped cream over the top. Sprinkle with the crushed candy. Spoon the chocolate sauce into a small sealable bag and cut off a tiny corner of the bag. Drizzle the chocolate sauce over the top of the cake. Chill for 8 hours before serving.

NOTE: *Be sure to serve the cake quickly, as the whipped cream will soften once removed from the refrigerator. If you are trying to cut calories, you can sugar substitute for the sugar. You can also try other variations on the cake. Use almond, coconut, vanilla, or cherry extract, making sure to switch the food coloring to an appropriate color. Try substituting other flavors for the chocolate mint cookies. Try vanilla wafers, orange extract, and red and yellow food coloring to make an "orange creamsicle" version of the dessert.*

Graeter's, founded in Cincinnati in 1870 by Louis C. Graeter, employs the "French Pot" process of making ice cream, which, along with their handmade chocolate candies and baked goods, is a tradition in Cincinnati. The premium ice cream is made by freezing it in a chilled, spinning French pot. The chocolate chip variations are made by pouring liquid chocolate into the pot and allowing it freeze into a thin shell on top of the ice cream. A blade is used to break up the shell. It is then mixed into the ice cream, making the huge dark chocolate chips for which Graeter's is famous. The Graeter family continues to make the ice cream, which has been featured on the Food Network and is a favorite of Oprah Winfrey, in small two-gallon batches. The premium ice cream is thick and creamy and comes in a variety of flavors.

Cincinnati Seasoned

Hot Chocolate Mousse

Serves 6

This recipe puts a new spin on the classic chocolate mousse dessert. The chili powder offers a surprising kick, making it the perfect compliment that's sure to please your sweet tooth.

6 tablespoons very strong brewed coffee
1/4 cup coffee liqueur
1 cup (6 ounces) dark chocolate chips
2 cups heavy whipping cream
3 tablespoons confectioners' sugar
Chocolate Cups (see Note)
1/2 teaspoon chili powder

Mix the coffee and liqueur in a bowl. Melt the chocolate chips in a saucepan over low heat. Whisk the melted chocolate into the coffee mixture and let cool to room temperature. Beat the whipping cream and confectioners' sugar in a large mixing bowl until soft peaks form. Add the chocolate mixture and beat until firm but not grainy; do not overbeat. Chill for up to 2 hours. Spoon into Chocolate Cups or wine glasses and sprinkle with the chili powder.

NOTE: *To make Chocolate Cups, blow up six small balloons to the size of an orange. Dip one-half of each balloon into melted chocolate chips to coat, holding the balloon at the tied end. Place the balloons chocolate side down on a baking sheet lined with waxed paper. Chill for 10 minutes or until the chocolate is hard. Prick the balloons with a pin to deflate and peel the balloon from the chocolate cup. Chill the cups until ready to serve.*

Kahlúa Parfaits
Serves 8

1 (8-ounce) package chocolate-covered toffee bits
3 pints coffee ice cream, softened
1 cup Kahlúa
1/2 cup whipped cream or whipped topping
8 sprigs of mint for garnish
2/3 cup fresh raspberries for garnish

Spoon 1 tablespoon of the toffee bits into the bottom of each of eight parfait glasses and add one-third cup ice cream to each glass. Drizzle 1 tablespoon Kahlúa into each glass. Repeat the layers, using about one-half cup ice cream in each glass. Freeze the parfaits for 5 to 10 minutes. Spoon 1 tablespoon of the whipped cream on top of each parfait and sprinkle with the remaining toffee bits. Garnish each parfait with a mint sprig and a few raspberries and serve. These may be prepared up to 2 days in advance. Store in the freezer until ready to serve.

NOTE: *Chocolate-covered toffee bits are found in the baking aisle near the chocolate chips. If not available, you may chop chocolate-covered toffee bars with a knife.*

Blackberry Meringue

Serves 6 to 8

1 tablespoon superfine sugar
1 tablespoon cornstarch
1/2 teaspoon white vinegar
3 egg whites, at room temperature
1/2 cup plus 3 tablespoons superfine sugar
1 1/2 cups heavy whipping cream
2 tablespoons confectioners' sugar (optional)
1 pound blackberries or other soft fruit
1/2 cup heavy whipping cream

Preheat the oven to 275 degrees. Mix 1 tablespoon superfine sugar, cornstarch and vinegar in a small bowl. Beat the egg whites with an electric whisk in a mixing bowl until stiff. Beat in 11 tablespoons superfine sugar slowly. Beat in the cornstarch mixture. Draw an 8- to 10-inch circle on a sheet of waxed paper on a baking sheet. Spread the egg white mixture over the circle, mounding the edges higher than the center to form a nest. Bake for 1 hour. Turn off the heat and let the meringue cool slowly in the oven, making certain it does not brown. Remove the waxed paper carefully and place the meringue on a serving plate. Beat 1 1/2 cups whipping cream in a mixing bowl until soft peaks form. Beat in the confectioners' sugar. Spread one-half of the blackberries over the meringue. Spread the whipped cream over the berries and top with the remaining berries. Cut into wedges and serve with 1/2 cup whipping cream.

NOTE: *You may bake the meringue in advance and store, wrapped in waxed paper in an airtight container, for up to 48 hours or freeze for up to one month. This recipe is perfect for making individual servings, which may be easier, especially if you are preparing this recipe for a dinner party. Reduce your baking time accordingly and spread the other filling ingredients over eight small meringues. Use what you need and freeze the rest.*

The place of many historical beginnings, Cincinnati in 1850 was the first city in the United States to establish a Jewish Hospital. It is also where America's first municipal fire department was established in 1853

Fresh Blueberry Crisp

Serves 6

4 cups blueberries

1 cup all-purpose flour

1 cup packed brown sugar

$^1/2$ cup rolled oats

$^1/2$ teaspoon cinnamon

$^1/4$ teaspoon ginger

1 dash of salt

$^1/2$ cup (1 stick) butter

Whipped cream (optional)

Grated lemon zest (optional)

Preheat the oven to 400 degrees. Spread the berries in a buttered 9×9-inch baking dish. Combine the flour, brown sugar, oats, cinnamon, ginger and salt in a bowl and mix well. Cut in the butter with a pastry blender until crumbly. Sprinkle over the berries. Bake for 25 to 30 minutes or until light brown. Cool for 15 minutes. Spoon into serving bowls and top with whipped cream and lemon zest.

Pear Custard Tart

Serves 6

2 egg yolks

3 tablespoons cornstarch

1 tablespoon granulated sugar

1 cup milk

2 tablespoons orange marmalade

1 baked (7-inch) pie shell

2 pears, sliced

Confectioners' sugar

Sliced almonds

Combine the egg yolks, cornstarch, granulated sugar and milk in the top of a double boiler and mix well. Cook over simmering water until thickened, stirring constantly. Remove the top of the double boiler and let cool. Spread the marmalade over the bottom of the pie shell. Arrange the pear slices over the marmalade. Pour the cooled custard evenly over the pears and sprinkle with confectioners' sugar and almonds. Place under the broiler until light brown; serve immediately.

Desserts

Savannah Peach Cobbler

Serves 6

This easy recipe is sure to please on a hot summer day.

16 ounces sliced peeled peaches
1 cup sugar
1/2 cup (1 stick) butter
1 1/2 cups all-purpose flour
1/2 cup sugar
2 teaspoons baking powder
1 pinch of salt
1/2 cup milk

Preheat the oven to 350 degrees. Mix the peaches and 1 cup sugar in a bowl and set aside. Melt the butter in a 4×8-inch loaf dish in the oven. Combine the flour, 1/2 cup sugar, the baking powder, salt and milk in a bowl and mix well. Spoon over the melted butter in the loaf dish; do not stir. Spoon the peaches over the batter. Bake for 45 to 60 minutes or until golden brown.

NOTE: *For a variation on this classic dessert, add 16 ounces cherries and 1 teaspoon cinnamon to the peaches. Or, feel free to use mixed berries or blueberries instead of peaches. You can also substitute whole wheat flour for all-purpose flour and use skim milk instead of whole milk.*

The Junior League of Cincinnati moved into Columbia Center on June 25, 1988, in 103-degree heat. The grand ol' building was showing her use and her age. Investing $1.5 million in renovations, JLC now has much more than just a building— we have a home.

Peanut Butter Pie

Serves 8

1 1/2 cups all-purpose flour
2 tablespoons granulated sugar
1/2 teaspoon salt
1/2 cup vegetable oil
2 tablespoons milk
8 ounces cream cheese, softened
1/2 cup chunky peanut butter
1 cup confectioners' sugar
1/2 cup milk
8 ounces whipped topping
1/2 cup (3 ounces) semisweet chocolate chips
1/4 cup half-and-half
1/4 cup light corn syrup
1/8 teaspoon cream of tartar
1/2 cup salted peanuts, finely chopped
3 to 4 tablespoons half-and-half

Preheat the oven to 400 degrees. Combine the flour, granulated sugar, salt, oil and 2 tablespoons milk in a bowl and mix well. Form into a ball. Roll into a circle on a lightly floured surface and fit into a 9-inch pie plate. Bake for 10 to 12 minutes. Remove to a wire rack to cool. Beat the cream cheese in a mixing bowl until light and fluffy. Beat in the peanut butter and confectioners' sugar. Beat in 1/2 cup milk. Fold in the whipped topping. Pour into the cooled crust and freeze until firm.

Combine the chocolate chips, 1/4 cup half-and-half, the corn syrup, cream of tartar and peanuts in a saucepan. Cook, covered, over low heat for 10 minutes. Uncover and cook until the chocolate is melted, stirring constantly. Remove from the heat and let cool. Chill in the refrigerator until cold. Stir in 3 to 4 tablespoons half-and-half to reach the desired consistency. Place the pie in the refrigerator 30 minutes before serving. Cut the pie into slices and serve with the chocolate peanut sauce.

NOTE: *You may warm the chocolate sauce before serving, if desired.*

Ice Cream Pie

Serves 6

2 cups graham cracker crumbs
2 tablespoons sugar
1/2 cup (1 stick) butter, melted
2 (3-ounce) packages French vanilla
    instant pudding mix
2 cups milk

1 quart butter pecan ice cream,
    softened
3 5th Avenue candy bars, chopped
8 ounces whipped topping
3 5th Avenue candy bars, chopped

Combine the graham cracker crumbs, sugar and butter in a bowl and mix well. Press over the bottom and up the side of a 9-inch pie plate. Combine the pudding mix, milk, softened ice cream and three candy bars in a bowl and mix well. Spoon into the prepared crust. Freeze for 1 hour. Spread the whipped topping over the pie and sprinkle with three candy bars.

Cheese and Apple Cake

Serves 4

This sticky cake is a play on two flavor combinations that are a hit during hors d'oeuvre. Now you can treat your guests to cheese and apples for dessert!

2 Gala or red Delicious apples,
    peeled and sliced
1/2 cup (1 stick) butter, softened
1/2 cup sugar
2 eggs

1 cup self-rising flour
1/2 cup raisins
4 ounces grated cheese,
    such as Lancashire

Preheat the oven to 350 degrees. Microwave the apples in a microwave-safe bowl on High for 3 minutes or until soft; cool. Combine the butter, sugar, eggs and flour in a bowl and mix well. Stir in the apples. Spread the raisins over the bottom of a greased and floured 8×8-inch baking pan. Spread the batter evenly over the raisins. Bake for 30 to 45 minutes or until the cake tests done. Remove to a wire rack to cool. Invert the cake onto a work surface and cut the cake in half horizontally. Place the bottom half of the cake on a serving plate, cut side up, and sprinkle with the cheese. Top with the remaining cake half. Chill until ready to serve.

Rich and Sinful Chocolate Cake

Serves 8

1 cup buttermilk
1 teaspoon baking soda
1 cup (2 sticks) butter, softened
2 cups sugar
4 eggs
2¹/₂ cups cake flour
4 ounces German's sweet
   chocolate, melted

¹/₃ cup hot water
1 teaspoon vanilla extract
¹/₈ teaspoon salt
Rich and Sinful Chocolate Icing
   (below)

Preheat the oven to 325 degrees. Mix the buttermilk and baking soda in a small bowl. Beat the butter and sugar in a mixing bowl until light and fluffy. Add the eggs one at a time, beating well after each addition. Beat in the buttermilk mixture alternately with the flour one-third at a time, beating well after each addition. Beat in the chocolate, water, vanilla and salt. Pour into a greased and floured 9×13-inch baking pan. Bake for 30 minutes. Increase the heat to 350 degrees and bake until a wooden pick inserted into the center comes out clean. Remove to a wire rack to cool. Ice with Rich and Sinful Chocolate Icing.

NOTE: *If you do not have cake flour, use all-purpose flour, removing 2 tablespoons per cup of flour.*

Rich and Sinful Chocolate Icing

Makes about 2 cups

¹/₂ cup (1 stick) butter
¹/₂ cup milk
¹/₂ cup baking cocoa

2 cups sugar
1 teaspoon vanilla extract

Combine the butter and milk in a heavy saucepan and cook until the butter is melted. Mix the baking cocoa and sugar together and stir into the milk mixture. Bring to a boil and cook for 2 minutes without stirring. Stir and remove from the heat. Stir in the vanilla and let cool until beginning to thicken. Beat until smooth. Spread over Rich and Sinful Chocolate Cake before the icing cools completely and hardens.

Cincinnati Seasoned

Bonfire Night Sponge Parkin
Serves 8

Parkin is a soft cake traditionally eaten on Bonfire Night, also known as Guy Fawkes Night in Great Britain. The holiday celebrates the foiling of a plot to blow up the British House of Parliament.

2 cups all-purpose flour
1 cup sugar
1^{1}/2 teaspoons ginger
^{1}/2 cup (1 stick) unsalted butter

1 cup milk, warmed
^{1}/2 teaspoon baking soda
2 tablespoons maple syrup
1 egg, beaten

Preheat the oven to 350 degrees. Combine the flour, sugar and ginger in a bowl and mix well. Cut in the butter with a pastry blender until crumbly. Mix the milk, baking soda and maple syrup in a bowl. Add to the flour mixture and beat well. Add the egg and beat well. Pour into a greased and floured 9×13-inch baking pan. Bake for 1 hour or until the top springs back when lightly touched and the cake is pulling away from the edge. Remove to a wire rack to cool completely. Cut into squares and serve.

Moist Gingerbread Cake
Serves 6

2^{1}/2 cups all-purpose flour
1 teaspoon baking soda
2 teaspoons ginger
2 teaspoons cinnamon
^{1}/2 cup packed brown sugar

^{1}/2 cup (1 stick) butter or margarine
^{3}/4 cup black treacle or dark molasses
^{3}/4 cup maple syrup
^{1}/2 cup water
2 eggs, beaten

Preheat the oven to 350 degrees. Combine the flour, baking soda, ginger, cinnamon and brown sugar in a food processor and pulse to mix. Heat the butter, treacle and maple syrup in a saucepan until the butter is melted, stirring constantly. Remove from the heat and stir in the water. Stir in the eggs gradually. Add the egg mixture to the food processor, processing constantly until well mixed. Pour into a greased and floured 10×10-inch baking pan. Bake for 45 minutes or until a wooden pick inserted into the center comes out clean. Remove to a wire rack to cool.

"The Wizard of Oz," presented by the Players of the Junior League of Cincinnati—1925–1926

Apple Squares

Serves 12

*This is a perfect alternative to whip up the next time your
children are begging for brownies.*

1 cup all-purpose flour
1 teaspoon baking powder
1/4 teaspoon salt
1/4 teaspoon cinnamon
1/4 cup (1/2 stick) unsalted butter, melted and
   slightly cooled
1/2 cup packed light brown sugar
1/2 cup granulated sugar
1 egg
1 teaspoon vanilla extract
1/2 cup chopped apple
1/2 cup finely chopped walnuts or other nuts (optional)
1 tablespoon Cinnamon-Sugar Topping

Preheat the oven to 350 degrees. Sift the flour, baking powder, salt and
cinnamon together. Beat the butter, brown sugar, granulated sugar, egg and vanilla
in a mixing bowl until smooth. Stir in the dry ingredients just until mixed. Stir in
the apple and walnuts. Spread into a greased 8×8-inch baking pan. Sprinkle with
the Cinnamon-Sugar Topping. Bake for 30 minutes or until the top springs back
when lightly touched. Remove to a wire rack to cool completely. Cut into squares
and serve.

NOTE: *Be sure to chop the apples an appropriate size. If they are too large, they will
not cook well. If they are too small, they will disappear! You can double the recipe
and bake as muffins instead of using a baking pan.*

*To make Cinnamon-Sugar
Topping, combine 1/2 cup
sugar and 1 1/2 teaspoons
cinnamon in a bowl
and mix well. Store in
an airtight container.
Use to make cinnamon
toast or sprinkle on
French toast.*

Desserts

Oatmeal Chocolate Bars

Serves 12 to 16

1 cup (2 sticks) unsalted
   butter, softened
1/2 cup packed light brown sugar
1/2 cup granulated sugar
2 egg yolks

1 cup sifted all-purpose flour
1 cup rolled oats
6 (1 1/2-ounce) chocolate candy bars
Coarsely chopped pecans to taste

Preheat the oven to 350 degrees. Beat the butter, brown sugar and granulated sugar in a mixing bowl until light and fluffy. Beat in the egg yolks. Mix the flour and oats in a bowl. Add to the butter mixture and mix well. Press over the bottom of a greased and floured 9×13-inch baking pan. Bake for 20 minutes. Arrange the candy bars over the crust. Bake for 2 to 3 minutes longer or until the chocolate is partially melted. Spread the chocolate evenly over the crust and sprinkle with pecans. Cool completely before cutting into squares.

Caramel-Filled Chocolate Cookies

Makes about 40 cookies

These delightful chocolate cookies are great for holiday parties, or
serve them right out of the oven for an ooey, gooey treat.

2 1/2 cups all-purpose flour
3/4 cup baking cocoa
1 teaspoon baking soda
2 cups (4 sticks) butter or
   margarine, softened
1 cup granulated sugar

1 cup packed brown sugar
2 eggs
2 teaspoons vanilla extract
1 bag chocolate-covered
   caramels, unwrapped
Additional granulated sugar

Preheat the oven to 375 degrees. Mix the flour, baking cocoa and baking soda together. Beat the butter, 1 cup granulated sugar and the brown sugar in a mixing bowl until light and fluffy. Beat in the eggs and vanilla. Beat in the dry ingredients gradually; the dough will be slightly sticky. Add a very small amount of water if the dough seems too dry. Shape a small amount of dough around each caramel to cover, using floured hands, to make balls no larger than 1 1/2 inches in diameter. Roll the balls in additional granulated sugar and place on a nonstick cookie sheet. Bake for 7 to 10 minutes or until the tops are slightly cracked. Cool on the cookie sheet for 5 minutes. Remove to a wire rack to cool.

Cincinnati Seasoned

Cowboy Cookies

Makes 4 dozen cookies

*This cookie is a fan favorite for all ages! The toffee bits are a must—
they provide a bit of crunch and a sweet caramel touch.*

1 1/2 cups all-purpose flour
1 teaspoon baking soda
1/2 teaspoon salt
1 cup (2 sticks) unsalted butter, softened
1 cup packed light brown sugar
1/2 cup granulated sugar
2 eggs
1 teaspoon vanilla extract
3 cups rolled oats
1 cup dried cranberries
1 cup flaked coconut
1 cup chocolate-covered toffee bits

Preheat the oven to 350 degrees. Mix the flour, baking soda and salt together. Beat the butter, brown sugar and granulated sugar in a mixing bowl until light and fluffy. Beat in the eggs and vanilla. Beat in the dry ingredients. Add the oats and cranberries and stir just until mixed. Add the coconut and toffee bits and stir just until mixed. Drop by rounded tablespoonfuls onto an ungreased cookie sheet. Bake for 10 to 12 minutes or until golden brown. Cool on the cookie sheet for 1 minute. Remove to a wire rack to cool completely.

NOTE: *Be sure not to overmix the dough or it will become stiff. You only want to stir until those final few ingredients are incorporated. If using an electric mixer, switch to a wooden spoon when adding the oats, cranberries, coconut, and toffee bits.*

General Arthur St. Clair, governor of the Northwest Territory, named Cincinnati in honor of the Roman citizen-soldier Lucius Quinctius Cincinnatus and also after the Society of the Cincinnati, an organization of American Revolutionary army officers.

Desserts

Triple Chocolate Chip Cookies

Makes 5 dozen cookies

2 1/4 cups all-purpose flour

1 teaspoon baking soda

1 teaspoon salt

1 cup (2 sticks) butter, softened

2 cups granulated sugar

2 cups packed brown sugar

2 teaspoons vanilla extract

2 eggs

2 cups rolled oats or quick-cooking oats

1 1/2 cups (9 ounces) each semisweet
  chocolate chips, white chocolate
  chips and milk chocolate chunks

1/2 cup chopped nuts

Preheat the oven to 350 degrees. Mix the flour, baking soda and salt together. Beat the butter, granulated sugar, brown sugar and vanilla in a mixing bowl until light and fluffy. Add the eggs one at a time beating well after each addition. Beat in the dry ingredients gradually. Stir in the oats, semisweet chocolate chips, white chocolate chips, milk chocolate chunks and nuts. Drop by rounded tablespoonfuls onto an ungreased cookie sheet. Bake for 12 to 15 minutes or until golden brown. Cool on the cookie sheet for 2 minutes. Remove to a wire rack to cool completely.

Soft and Moist Pumpkin Cookies

Makes 40 cookies

*When the smell of autumn is in the air, these pumpkin
cookies will get you into the fall spirit.*

2 cups all-purpose flour

2 teaspoons baking powder

1 teaspoon cinnamon

1/2 teaspoon salt

1 cup canned pumpkin

1 cup sugar

1/2 cup vegetable oil

1 egg

1 teaspoon baking soda

1 teaspoon milk

1 cup milk chocolate chips or raisins

1 teaspoon vanilla extract

1/2 cup chopped nuts (optional)

Preheat the oven to 375 degrees. Mix the flour, baking powder, cinnamon and salt together. Combine the pumpkin, sugar, oil and egg in a bowl and mix well. Stir in the dry ingredients. Dissolve the baking soda in the milk in a small bowl; stir into the pumpkin mixture. Stir in the chocolate chips, vanilla and nuts. Drop by teaspoonfuls onto a lightly greased cookie sheet. Bake for 10 to 12 minutes or until light brown. Cool on the cookie sheet for 2 minutes. Remove to a wire rack to cool completely.

Cincinnati Seasoned

Chocolate Toffee Grahams

Makes 12 dozen

1 (14-ounce) box graham crackers
1 cup (2 sticks) butter
1 cup packed brown sugar
1/4 cup your favorite chopped nuts
2 cups (12 ounces) semisweet chocolate chips

Preheat the oven to 350 degrees. Fit the graham crackers tightly in a single layer in a greased 10×15-inch baking pan; reserve any unused crackers for another use. Bring the butter and brown sugar to a boil in a saucepan. Boil for 2 minutes, stirring constantly. Pour evenly over the graham crackers and sprinkle with the nuts. Bake for 7 minutes. Sprinkle the chocolate chips over the warm layers; spread the melted chocolate evenly over the nuts. Cut into 1-inch squares while warm and let cool in the pan. Store in a tightly covered container in the refrigerator.

Graham Cracker Cookies

Makes 4 dozen

24 cinnamon graham crackers
1/2 cup (1 stick) butter
1/2 cup (1 stick) margarine
1 cup packed light brown sugar
1 cup chopped nuts

Preheat the oven to 350 degrees. Fit the graham crackers tightly in a single layer in a 10×15-inch baking pan lined with foil. Melt the butter and margarine in a saucepan and stir in the brown sugar. Bring to a boil and cook for 2 minutes, stirring constantly. Pour evenly over the graham crackers and sprinkle with the nuts. Bake for 12 minutes. Cut into squares while hot and let cool in the pan.

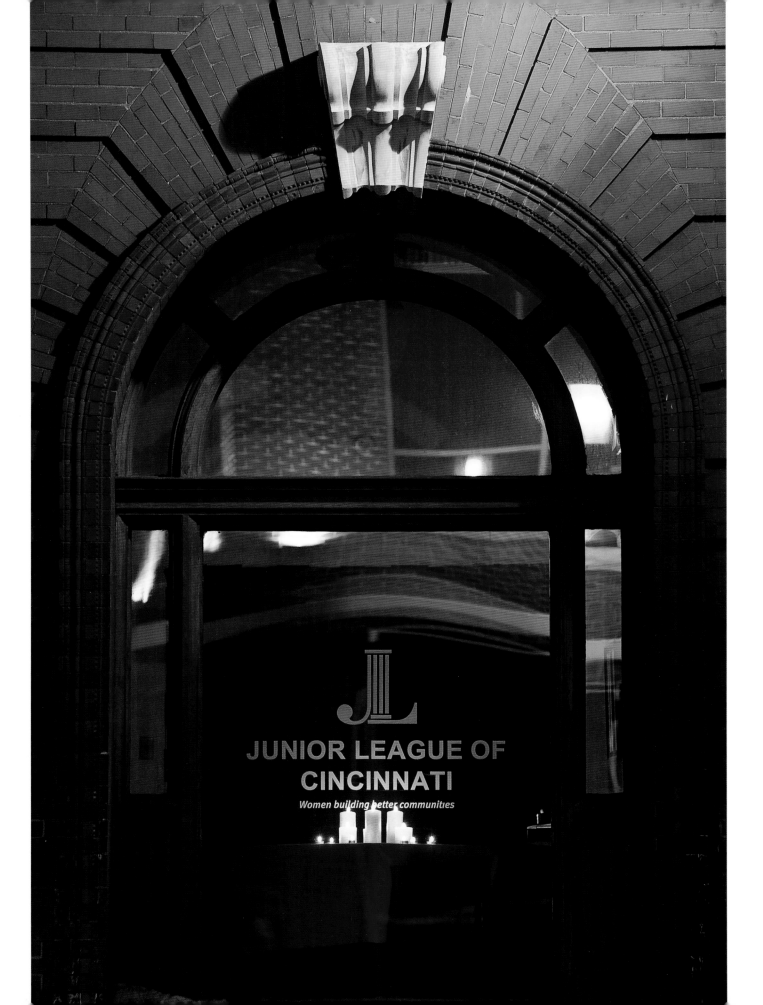

Enclosures

Columbia Center

It was day in September 1904, and a community celebration was taking place. An impressive three-story, red brick building with a large window, elegant lighting fixtures, and a main door facing Columbia Parkway was the center of attention. It was the Grand Ceremony opening the Yeatman Masonic Temple. Large assembly rooms occupied the first and second floors. The first floor also had a stage large enough to handle small plays. The second floor had a smaller stage suitable for the Mason's formal meetings. Most impressive were the large figures made of stained glass looking out on Columbia Tusculm.

Seventy-five years later, the Columbia Auction Gallery occupied this beautiful building, allowing buyers from all over the tri-state area to visit its first-floor bidding hall. The Columbia Parkway entrance was remade into an attractive window and ten-foot-high wooden doors became the entrance for customers.

The Junior League of Cincinnati moved into the Columbia Center on June 25, 1988, in 103-degree heat. The grand ol' building was showing her use and her age. With $1.5 million to renovate, JLC now has much more that just a building, we have a home. For more information on Junior League of Cincinnati, including our mission, past and present projects, and membership, please visit www.jlcincinnati.org.

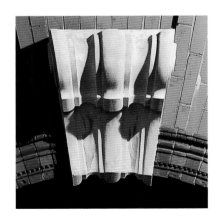

From the Photographer

Photography took hold of me many years ago. It seemed to be the best way to convey my view of the world not only to others, but to myself. It is the center of my world.

Through some beautiful twist of fate I was selected to do the photography for the Junior League of Cincinnati's new cookbook. Their concept to present food, various landmarks, and views of the city in the same image was bold and ambitious. The sheer variety of locations gave us many challenges. But it was, for me, the most rewarding and fun photography project.

A special thanks to the talented people who helped me in the completion of this most gratifying project.

Wendy Ramsey—Photo Assistant
Brian Herrmann—Photo Assistant
Gene Fischer—Photo Assistant
Jason Lykins—Photo Assistant
Aaron Asch—Photo Retouching

Special thanks (she knows why) to Candice DeClark Peace, CPA and financial advisor with Clark, Schaeffer, Hackett & Co.

And a standing ovation from me to Katy Crossen and the women of the Junior League of Cincinnati. The book you hold in your hands was accomplished through the vision of this group. It showcases all the long history and mission of the Junior League and the bounty of life in the Cincinnati area.

Shad Ramsey
Ramsey Photography
www.shadramsey.com

Special Acknowledgments

Photography—Shad Ramsey of Shad Ramsey Photography
ramseyphoto@hotmail.com or 513-418-1754

Food stylist—Chef Renée Schuler of Eat Well LLC
www.eatwellonline.com or 513-515-0998

Special Thanks

Christina Anderson and Valentine Nastor of Cincinnati Zoo and Botanical Garden

Michael Anderson of the Cincinnati Reds/Great American Ball Park

Jeff Berding and Ellen Ritter of the Cincinnati Bengals/Paul Brown Stadium

Kathy Comisar of Corporex and The Ascent at Roebling Bridge

Anthony Gregory of Junior League of Cincinnati

Chad Mertz of Cincinnati Museum Center at Union Terminal

Scott Mescher of Drees Pavilion at Devou Park, City of Covington Parks

David Millett of David A. Millett, Inc.

Andrea Schepmann of Krohn Conservatory and the City of Cincinnati
     Parks Department

Preeti Thakar and Amy Burke of Cincinnati Art Museum

Donna and Roger Weddle of Wiedemann Hill Mansion

Tablescape Locations, Designers, and Sponsors

Cover, Drees Pavilion at Devou Park: Page Hall of Hall Design Group

Page 10, Great American Ball Park: Tiffany and Jeremy Heath

Page 36, Paul Brown Stadium: Tiffany Heath of NCIM

Page 44, The Ascent at Roebling Bridge: Chef Renee Schuler of Eat Well

Page 56, Wiedemann Hill Mansion: Donna Weddle

Page 66, Cincinnati Museum Center at Union Terminal: Erin Lombardi
     of Closson's

Page 92, Krohn Conservatory: Kirsten Kulkarni of Eclectique Home Décor

Page 134, Elephant House at Cincinnati Zoo: Christina Anderson, designer;
     Valentine Nastor, elephant coordinator

Page 154, Tyler Davidson Fountain at Fountain Square: Cookbook Committee

Page 180, Junior League of Cincinnati Columbia Center: Katy Crossen

Recipe Contributors

Christina Anderson

Tracy Athan

Melanie Atkinson

Lisa Baker

Tiffany Boyd

Vicki Marsala Calonge

Leslie Cannon

Mary-Kate Carpenter

Stephanie Chapman

Melanie M. Chavez

Caroline Colvin

Carolyn Cox

Ann K. Crossen

Katy Crossen

Tiffiny Grale Dawson

Margaret Denham

Maggie DePowell

Amanda Diers

Heather Egan

Jeff Eggleston

Kim Emmer

Natalie Etienne

MaryEllen Farrell

Brigid Crossen Fintak

Steve Fintak

Amy Wright Flischel

Susan Fraley

Harriet D. French

Shelli French

Jeff Glaspie

Meredith Gorentz

Sara Gouedy

Stephanie Greis

Sarah Grimmer

Susie Guggenheim

Lisa R. Martin Hawver

Tiffany Heath

Lauren Heis

Erin Herring

Brooke Hiltz

Lisa Hubbard

Irene Ingham

Heather Jackson

Amy Kattman

Dorian Kern

Jennifer Kinnen

Meredith Koch

Jane Koppenhoefer

Chris Kritikos

Allison Lied

Beth Locaputo

Jean Long

Wendy Rosekrans Marik

Kenneth Minkove

Kate Molinsky

Sarah Moore

Elizabeth Ogle

Jennifer Reed

Jennifer Schlotman

Chef Renée Schuler

Julie Cayse Sevachko

Jessica Shelly

Emily Shewmaker

Donna Shirley

Deanna Sicking

Alizha V. Smith

Linda J. Smith

Alison Smythe

Liz Stoffregen

Carolyn Taylor

Preeti Joshi Thakar

Elizabeth L. Holman
    Vainrib

Nancy Van Epps

Brigid Williamson

Pamela Wise

Jill Wittman

Meredith Yacso

Dinese Young

Kimberly Young

"The Wizard of Oz," presented by the Players of the Junior League of Cincinnati—1925–1926

Index

Cincinnati Seasoned

Index

Index

Cincinnati Seasoned

Index

Index

Index

Cincinnati Seasoned

Ingredient Assumptions

The following are intended to help you when preparing our recipes.

Eggs are large unless another size is specified in the recipe. To avoid raw eggs that may carry salmonella, use an equivalent amount of commercial egg substitute.

Milk is whole unless otherwise stated.

Margarine for cooking is hard (baking) margarine, not soft or light.

Ingredients in cans or jars are undrained unless the recipe specifies draining.

Vegetables and fruits are fresh unless specified differently.

Vegetables and fruits are of medium size unless another size is specified.

Horseradish and mustard are prepared unless specified differently.

For additional copies of

Cincinnati Seasoned
Savoring the Queen City's Spice of Life

please visit our Web site, www.jlcincinnati.org, or telephone Junior League of Cincinnati at 513-871-9339.